Copyright © 2005 by Bob Doll

All rights reserved. No part of this book shall be reproduced or transmitted in any form or by any means, electronic, mechanical, magnetic, photographic including photocopying, recording or by any information storage and retrieval system, without prior written permission of the publisher. No patent liability is assumed with respect to the use of the information contained herein. Although every precaution has been taken in the preparation of this book, the publisher and author assume no responsibility for errors or omissions. Neither is any liability assumed for damages resulting from the use of the information contained herein.

ISBN 0-7414-2720-6

The stories are true. Some of the names have been omitted or changed to protect the guilty.

Published by:

INFINITY
PUBLISHING.COM

1094 New DeHaven Street, Suite 100
West Conshohocken, PA 19428-2713
Info@buybooksontheweb.com
www.buybooksontheweb.com
Toll-free (877) BUY BOOK
Local Phone (610) 941-9999
Fax (610) 941-9959

Printed in the United States of America
Printed on Recycled Paper
Published December 2005

The RADIO FUNNY Book

By

Bob Doll

*Jim T,
All The Best
Bob Doll
2-17-06*

To Barbara,
who's made this
effort possible

CONTENTS

Foreword i
1. Meet the Man on the Street 1
2. Man on the Street Flashbacks 4
3. Now You're Talkin' 8
4. Starting Out 14
5. Going to the Fair 19
6. From TV to Radio 20
7. Take Me Out to the Ballgame 24
8. A Lotta' Laughs 27
9. Detour Back to Radio History 29
10. What Do Those Letters Mean? 32
11. Echoes of Border Radio 36
12. It Made You Feel Real Good 38
13. Fun and Games 40
14. Radio "Q" and "A" 50
15. Go Football! Go! 52
16. In the Public Interest 57
17. Beyond the Call of Duty 60
18. A Word from Our Sponsor 62
19. Radio Announcer Test 67
20. Selling Radio Advertising 68
21. Inside Stuff 75
22. Getting Fired 83

23. Getting Hired 89
24. Let's Play Basketball 93
25. We've Got News for You 95
26. Radio Personalities 99
27. We Now Leave Our Studios 102
28. Radio Hoaxes 108
29. Losing It 113
30. The Radio Show Must Go On 116
31. Radio's Disc Jockeys 122
32. The Miss Parade 128
33. Politics 132
34. Radio Politicians 134
35. Politics Almost Ended It 136
36. Sports Miscellany 138
37. From the Radio Sports Scrapbook 142
38. Uncle Don 143
39. It Slipped 145
Index 151

FOREWORD

Around 1950, when I got started in the radio business, a man, who had bought and "turned around" a little radio station in Colorado, wrote a book about his experience. I do not know the man's name and have never read his book. But, after 55 years in this business, I think the title of his book is the most appropriate phrase to describe all of us who have gotten into this business as performers or support, managers, even investors. His title? *I Bet My Shirt On the Wind.*

It takes an unusual kind of person to "make a bet" like that. The best radio folks I've known, and some not so gifted or lucky, all agree on one thing: This is above all a people business. These stories, therefore, deserve to be told. These are stories of radio people making fluffs and bloopers, and there are some people we catch "doing something right."

I have had a lot of encouragement to write this book. Art Sutton and Dean Sorenson have been particularly encouraging and supportive. I think they recognize this as respectable work for an old man.

This has been a "work in progress" of over two decades. The first person to suggest such a project to me was my longtime, close friend Bob Sherman,

A Big Ten football announcer (Ohio State and Michigan State University), he also did the play by play on the ABC Radio Network of the short-lived spring pro football league. Bob, a hugely talented radio man, died much too young—just 55.

It has been well said that radio is not really a career choice—it is a disease. Few people who are infected with it are ever cured. Even people who leave the business on less than happy terms continue to be fascinated by it and generally admit they miss it. No other line of work is quite as compelling as being in radio, which offers its practitioners more highs and lows than almost any other endeavor. No two days are ever alike. My friend Bob Sherman had the radio disease. He had a wonderful sense of humor about radio folks, including himself.

It was Bob who came up with the disclaimer, which appears with the title of this book: "The stories are true. Some of the names have been omitted or changed to protect the guilty."

Some of the stories you'll be reading here, you have heard before, or perhaps a very similar story. That's to be expected. When I got into the radio business, there were people in the stations who had "come aboard" in the 1920s and the '30s and '40s.

By temperament, they weren't much different than those of us who arrived in the 1950s and later. It was my good fortune to work in the Midwest and the South. I have friends and clients in the west and the east. Again, I don't find that much difference in radio people despite their geography.

I hope these stories will bring back some good memories for the radio people—present and past. I hope they will be a "fun read" for the folks outside radio who make it all possible: our customers and our listeners who pay attention to what we have to say and have to play.

The Book is Launched

One of the best pieces of advice I've ever gotten came from Bill Wertz at Kalamazoo, Michigan. I was associated part-time with him and Steve Trivers for five-and-a-half years in their program syndication and consulting business, "KalaMusic." Bill told me, "You don't have to bluff it. An intelligent person doesn't know everything, but he or she knows where to go to get information on how to solve a problem or realize an opportunity." When I undertook the writing of this book, I called a longtime friend, John Harris, who lives in Boca Raton, Florida. John and I were competitors back in the 1950s. He was editor of the local newspaper. I was manager of the town's radio station. The town was Cynthiana, Kentucky, between Cincinnati, Ohio, and Lexington, Kentucky.

The population was 4,900. The radio station I was running was as small as you could get—a 100 "watter."

I called John because I knew how much attention he paid to what was on WCYN. Among the services we offered was "Fire Calls." The fire station was a block from the radio station. When the fire whistle sounded, WCYN called to learn the location of the "fire run." The information was immediately broadcast with a message to listeners that following fire trucks was unsafe for the person doing it and the people fighting the fire. The "fire call" ended with a question asking listeners if they had had their property values brought up to date recently? They were then given the address and phone number of a local insurance agent who paid WCYN's highest minute rate—$3.00.

John and I were strong competitors. I always told him my job was much easier than his. His newspaper came out only on Wednesday afternoon. It could be carefully read in less than an hour. For him to keep up with me, he'd have to listen 17 hours a day, 7 days a week. I think he came close.

It might be called "collusion" now, but John and I socialized at least one late afternoon a week in a side-street tavern where we were unlikely to be seen by any of the town leaders. I can remember one afternoon a discussion of the county judge's bad luck—he'd been arrested for drunk driving. John and I both knew and liked him and knew he was making a valiant effort to get his drinking problem under control. We agreed that we wouldn't carry the story—after all, he hadn't hit anybody or anything.

Things were quiet for a couple of days, and then the story broke out in a fury. A preacher from a small conservative protestant church came on the station on Saturday morning with his regular weekly broadcast. He announced that his radio sermon topic would be, "Sober As A Judge." The young preacher not only described the county judge's drinking problem, but those of two other judges in town.

The following week, John's newspaper, *The Democrat*, carried a front-page picture of the judge fining himself the maximum. The caption read "HE TOOK IT LIKE A MAN." The judge continued to serve.

After his days at the weekly *Cynthiana Democrat*, John was for a time an entrepreneur serving as publisher of a weekly in a small Appalachian mountain town. John said after he sold out there, "The business aspects bored me. I wanted to get back on the beat." He landed a job on a metropolitan daily, *The Post* in Greater Cincinnati.

With the strict union work rules, he found himself with time on his hands and used that opportunity to freelance for the *National Enquirer*. Soon they made him an offer of fulltime employment. He says, "Making that change was a very simple one. The pay was twice what I was making, and the good weather was another very big plus."

When he made the decision to join the supermarket tabloid, he realized, "I was not going to be an award-winning journalist. Most people in the news business looked down on tabloids, but, I'll have to admit, covering humankind's eccentricities was a fun job. But, there were some frustrations. The paper was run like the smallest weekly in the country. It was a one-man show. That man was Generoso Pope—a man of, it seemed, unlimited wealth. He made every decision. Almost three quarters of the stories turned in by the reporters were never run. One such story, or series of stories, was "A Search for Utopia." Pope sent Harris out on a four-month search to look for "Utopia on Earth." His expenses totaled about $100,000. It did not run."

When a Mike Wallace staffer found out about the series that never made it to print, Wallace decided to do a "60 Minutes" piece on it. The filming was done in the *National Enquirer's* headquarters. Wallace opened his interview with, "Do you mean to tell me you spent four months and $100,000 worth of expense money on something that did not get printed?" John answered, "Yes" in a very respectful manner. That quarter hour on the highest rated TV show in the country back in the 1970s was worth a million dollars of free publicity.

"Pope was pretty shrewd, wasn't he?" John asks.

The 1970s were red-letter years for Pope and his publication. Newsstand sales were 5-million to 6-million a week. Beginning in the '80s, things started to tumble. There was more competition on the grocery store newsstands, and television had entered the field of what many called "trash journalism." The "tab" now has new owners and is being operated out of New York City.

John Harris, for his lifetime in journalism, does not have a Pulitzer Prize hanging over his mantle, but he says, "I've spent most of my time in the fun part of journalism, and I've got some pretty good assets in my safety deposit box, thanks to the good wages on the "Enquirer."

In retirement, he dabbles in public relations work when the jobs are "interesting." His occasional clients include boxing promoter Don King.

When I asked him to contribute some funny radio stories for this book, his #1 choice was an interview I conducted on my "street" show back in 1957. I asked an old country fellow what he was doing in town? His answer, "Just fartin' around."

I guess that's what I'm doing writing this book—and you're doing reading it. I hope it'll be a pleasant time for both of us.

MEET THE MAN ON THE STREET

In my early days in radio, the "Man on the Street" was my happiest chore. For 13 years, I did the program six days a week in five different towns. Like most activities in small towns, very little of note happened on the broadcasts. But, the programs were always among the most popular on the small stations where I cut my teeth on radio. That was also true on other stations, including 50,000-watt stations in cities of a half million.

The audience for "Man on the Street" programs no doubt tuned in "in case something happened." Maybe one of their neighbors would make a fool out of himself, or one of the officials who stopped by often would release some major news item prematurely.

When I decided to write this book, I told my friends up front, "I would tell some of my own embarrassing happenings. That's fair."

Ted Grizzard had perhaps the longest tenure as a radio man on the street in the business. He racked up 33 years, starting in 1936, winding up in 1969. Ted estimated he had done 8,488 "street broadcasts." I was surprised when he said in his memoir, *#1 is Chicken*, (publisher: Host), that he really didn't think most of the programs were "really very good." I'm sure his listeners didn't mind—they were waiting for "something special to happen." It did often enough to keep them listening.

In the book, Ted repeated what he thought was his best "interview." It is as follows:

"A middle-aged fellow, a bachelor, lived alone in the country. He'd stop by the 'street show' every now and then. He did his own cooking. Looked healthy. One day I asked him about his favorite item of food. He said immediately, 'cracklin soup.' Now cracklins I thought are dry meat skins. Most of the taste or flavor is already out of 'em. I pursued the soup thing and asked for the recipe.

"He said he put the cracklins in boiling water with salt and pepper and let 'em boil. When I expressed some doubt about the flavor, he said, 'Oh, I add lots of ketchup.' In case you'd like a copy of that recipe—there it is—cracklin' soup. You can ketchup it to your taste. In fact, the good thing about it is, you don't need the dern cracklins."

Looking back at my 13 years of "street" shows, I remember two all too well:

I was interviewing the wife of a rural mail carrier on WCSI, Columbus, Indiana. After a couple of preliminary questions, the following slipped out, "How long is your husband's route?" (Sounded like 'root' I'm afraid.)

The second interview I remember was on WEKY, Richmond, Kentucky, with a man who turned out to be a just released prison convict. I didn't ask him, he just volunteered the information. Before I could ask another question, he blurted out, "I'm on the way to find the guy who got me sent up." Over his shoulder, I noticed two uniformed police officers approaching us. With little fanfare, they ushered my radio interviewee into a cruiser and off to the police station. By making that threat on my program, he had violated the terms of his parole and was promptly returned to the state prison. I never saw him again and did not describe what had happened on the program. I was sure that somebody getting arrested on the program would discourage people from appearing.

The man on the street programs grew out of a 1932 program called "Sidewalk Interviews" on KTRH, Houston, Texas. By 1935, it was on a national network (NBC Blue) under the title "Vox Pop," "The Voice of the People." That network program was similar to ones being broadcast under theatre marquees and on busy street corners in all size towns on all size radio stations.

The authors of *Inside Talk Radio* tell of listening to a transcription of a 1936 "Vox Pop" broadcast. Passers-by were being asked about their opinions of the Landon-Roosevelt presidential election.

They were also being asked, "What's the difference between 'lingering' and 'loitering?'" None of those being interviewed had as clear an idea as the dictionary, which says: lingering is to persist or proceed slowly, to delay leaving. To loiter is to stand idly about, linger aimlessly. Delay or dawdle.

Parks Johnson and Jerry Belcher, who devised the program as "Sidewalk Interviews," believed that the average man or woman, selected at random, was just as interesting as the average celebrity, and he or she worked much cheaper. In 1932, interviewees were given $1.00. When the program went national on a network in 1935, there was an added prize. An alarm clock was set at the beginning of the show. The person being interviewed when the alarm went off was given an additional $5.00.

Parks Johnson stayed with the program. It was on well into the '40s. Parks never lost his belief in the program. For him, "It was always fun."

The "Man on the Street" has disappeared from the nation's Main Streets and radio stations for a good reason. There are just not enough people to linger or loiter by the microphone or their radio for such easygoing programs. Everybody concerned wants more action. What follows are those special occasions when somebody said something really funny on a "Man on the Street" program. It didn't happen often, but it was something very few people really wanted to miss.

MAN ON THE STREET FLASHBACKS

(Brutally Frank)

The Man on the Street stopped two old ladies to ask them what they were doing in town. One of them grabbed the microphone to relate: "Had to see the doctor. Can't pee."

Tom Webb, Retired Radio
Engineer, Dallas, Texas

From the same source, when he had to fill in for the regular "Man on the Street" during his days at WMST, Mount Sterling, Kentucky:

(Straight Political Talk)

An elderly gentleman approached the "Man on the Street," asking if he could say something about the governor's race. Tom replied, "Yes."

The old man said very loudly, "—is an SOB," but he didn't use the abbreviation.

(Daddy's Little Boy?)

KGW's Bob Tomlinson in Seattle, asked a 4-year-old boy, "What's your daddy's name?"

Answer: "Do you want my daddy's name or my momma's boyfriend's?"

Kermit Schafer
Prize Bloopers
Avenel Books
From his *All Time Great Bloopers*

(Knock On Wood)

Program host: "Are you a vegetarian, sir?"

Guest: "No, I'm a carpenter."

(Tough Question)

Some "Man on the Street," tried to get laughs by asking "trick questions." On a traveling "Man on the Street" show, which had stopped at Cynthiana, Kentucky, Ted Grizzard, stopped local merchant Abe Goldberg. He posed the following question to him:

"Is Mickey Mouse a dog or a cat?"

Abe's answer, "You thought you'd get me on that. He's a rabbit."

The incident in the 1940s made Abe mike shy the rest of his life. Whenever he'd see someone with a microphone, he crossed the street.

(Missing)

In Vidalia, Georgia, WVOP was doing a "Man on the Street" type broadcast from the local tobacco auction. Farmers were being interviewed about the sale of their crops.

When one of the farmers was asked, "How did your tobacco sale do?" The answer, "Not worth a damn. I lost my ass." The quick-thinking station announcer told his audience, "If you see a stray donkey, please call us at the radio station."

(Neither)

For years, Paul Hodges was one of Cincinnati's best-known radio personalities. He did a daily "Man on the Street" program during the noon hour from a downtown theatre lobby. He also did two programs a day interviewing travelers at the city's railroad station and at the bus station.

During his "Bus Time" program, Hodges noticed a man observing his broadcast with above average interest. Curiosity apparently got the best of Hodges, who with live microphone in hand approached the man with his "stock" opening question, "Are You Arriving or Leaving?" The guest promptly answered, "Neither!," handing him a summons to appear in Divorce Court.

(A Star Is Born)

In 1950, radio came to Bill Mack's tiny Texas hometown of Shamrock. Though he was still in his teens, Bill became a full-fledged staff member of KEVA's staff. The station was named for the owner's mother, whose picture hung prominently in the reception area.

Bill's duties included cleaning the station "john" and vacuuming the carpet. Being on the new station, as he was also, made him somewhat of a celebrity in town. In his "celebrity role," he invited one of the local girls to come to the station for a tour and to see him broadcasting. When she arrived with a girlfriend, he was in the rest room with the door open. He was on his knees cleaning the toilet with a brush. Not very glamorous.

A much more glamorous assignment was conducting the station's "Man on the Street" program from in front of a downtown restaurant. Bob Wills, the legendary Western music writer and performer appeared in Shamrock one evening. "The house" was packed. The next day, he slept in, showing up at noon at the restaurant in front of which Bill did his "street program."

With microphone in hand, young Bill Mack ambled inside and sat down at the counter next to Wills where he was

ZAPPA: "I guess you think that wooden leg makes you a table."

To a caller who had said something that he said offended him, Pyne said, "Go gargle with razor blades."

To a woman caller, he said, "Look lady. Every time you open your mouth, nothing but garbage falls out. Get off the phone, you creep!"

Pyne often said, "I have no respect for anyone who would appear on my program."

It was not Pyne's offensive manner or outrageous language that ended his spectacular career. His ratings stayed high until his sudden end. He was the victim of an untimely death by cancer. His syndicator had a million-dollar, life-insurance policy on him and retired on the proceeds.

(Before the Rush)

After Joe Pyne disappeared from talk radio, the format continued to grow but seemed to take on a more "service oriented" flavor. Programs centered on ethics and morality, relationships, health, mental health, auto and home repair, personal finance, and sports. There's also pleasant, informed conversation exemplified for two decades by Jim Bohannon. Many programs of that type remain on the air. They are not "talk radio's" marquee attractions or big moneymakers. They're just steady, reliable performers.

(The Rush Arrives)

In 1987, the Reagan administration let the "Fairness Doctrine" expire. No longer would stations have to give opposing sides an opportunity to answer one-sided political presentations. That made it possible for stations to broadcast the likes of Rush Limbaugh, Sean Hannity, Michael Savage,

Laura Ingrahm, Mike Gallagher, G. Gordon Liddy, etc. It's estimated they reach a combined weekly audience of over sixty million people. Critics often refer to talk radio as the "Right Wing Noise Machine."

In many markets, there are one, two, three "Right leaning" radio stations. But, there are still AM stations, and a few FM stations looking for a profitable format "hole." About a hundred stations nationwide at this writing are carrying what is called "progressive talk."

The "stars" of the new genre of radio talk offerings include: Al Franken, a comedian and best-selling author, formerly of "Saturday Night Live"; Ed Schultz, a former sports broadcaster, who comes from unlikely Fargo, North Dakota; and Jerry Springer who has diversified himself outside "trash TV" which has made him a multi-millionaire into a very serious liberal radio talk conductor.

(Not Funny)

The fact that "call-in talk shows" have a delay on them, prevents the kind of funny things happening that happened on "Man on the Street" programs. And, political talk show hosts take their programs and themselves very seriously. Their audiences are even more serious. If you don't believe that, go on the Internet to the "Web pages" maintained by talk show hosts of all political persuasions. You will find dozens of pieces of merchandise espousing the societal views the host and his listeners share. It's all first-class merchandise at prices quality offerings are expected to bring.

I have been told for years that there are two things you don't discuss in polite company: religion and politics. Talk radio has more than its share of detractors, but in truth, it is, while not perfect, a forum open to everyone to air his or her feelings on issues that profoundly affect his or her life. It is therefore a valuable asset in our democracy.

All but 4% of talk radio listeners are high school graduates or better. They are heavy consumers of all kinds of news media. Seventy-four percent voted in the 2004 presidential election ("Talkers' Magazine" research). They can't be dismissed as zanies.

(Listening in on Talk Radio)

"All of these rich guys like the Kennedy family and Perot, pretending to live just like we do, pretending to understand our trials and tribulations, and pretending to represent us, and they get away with this." The words are those of Rush Limbaugh, who makes over $30 million a year. By any measure, he is the mega star of talk radio. He modestly reminds his audience frequently.

Nationally syndicated Armstrong Williams, who identifies himself as a black conservative talk show host says, "There's more to life than conspiracy and hating White people and hating Jews."

On a Christian talk station in the "D.C. suburb" of Arlington, Virginia, a caller complains about the widespread availability of condoms, saying, "It seems we're trying to say, 'It's alright to be promiscuous if you do it right.'" He quickly adds, "It isn't!"

G. Gordon Liddy of Watergate infamy tells a listener, "I can cut the heart and sever the spine with one thrust of a two-edged stiletto."

On a single show, Don Imus called Newt Gingrich, "a man who would eat roadkill," O.J. Simpson, "a moron," Alice Rivlan, "a little dwarf," Bob Novak, "the man with the worst hair on the planet," and Ted Kennedy, "a fat slob with a head the size of a dumpster."

STARTING OUT

Most radio personalities get their start on one of the nation's small market stations. These stations are unrated, as Arbitron does not survey their audience extensively. Aspiring radio stars can most often get considered for a job there. The hours are long; the work (for radio work) is hard, and wages are meager.

Ray Livesay, who owned and operated radio stations in small Illinois, Ohio, and Florida towns, often told the story of interviewing a young man wanting to break into radio. When the applicant asked about fringe benefits and a retirement plan, Livesay advised, "We can offer you opportunity. If it's security you want, go down to the Post Office, they're probably accepting applications."

This book includes a lot of small-town radio stories because there are a lot of small-town stations (over half the total). Folks there are perfecting their skills, and embarrassing moments are not uncommon.

Basil Price spent twenty-seven years in small-town Kansas radio. He shares these stories:

A caller to a buy, sell, rent, trade program announced that she had three dog houses and a cat house for sale.

A local college student was doing the morning show for the first time. After talking about the beautiful sunrise, he proceeded to deliver the morning's farm news advising his listeners that 70% of the corn in Kansas had been manured instead of MATURED.

It is always good policy to read over an item before broadcasting it. Sometimes though, the small station announcer, with so many other chores to do, like answering the phone or collecting local news items, doesn't have the time. That's why you would have heard this on a Kansas station, "A deer crashed through a sliding glass door into a house. The deer ran all over the house doing much damage before leaving through the same door. THE DOOR LATER DIED."

From Kermit Shafer's "Prize Bloopers" (Fawcett World) is this commercial on a small-town station:

"That's the Willcox Drive-In on Highway 23. If you don't know where it's located—and—most people don't, it's so out of the way. I mean it's right on the highway. I mean next to the highway.

"Oh nuts. Just give me a call, and I'll take you out there."

From Francis Nash of WGOH/WUGO in Grayson, Kentucky:

"We used to play song dedications. It was pretty bad:

"This song is going out from Pam to Jerry. It's "Tennessee Stud" by Eddy Arnold. I guess she knows more about him than we do."

Also from Francis Nash:

"We had one announcer whose mouth and brain were not operating at the same speed. Example: instead of 10 o'clock and time to look at the weather, he said "It's ten o'clock and time to take a leak."

The same announcer on the station's for sale program announced:

"For sale: A two piece sexual couch instead of A TWO PIECE SECTIONAL COUCH."

Some years ago at a South Carolina station he was managing, Skeeter Dodd heard the following from a new announcer:

MUSIC: NEARER MY GOD TO THEE and fade for (in a somber voice). "It's time for the WAZE Obituary Report brought to you by Jenkins and Hanes Funeral Home." (name changed)

FADE MUSIC UP AND THEN FADE DOWN AGAIN: "We regret to announce there are no deaths to report today."

(Very Small Start)

Dean Sorenson who sold his small market chain of radio stations in the Upper Midwest for $28 million remembers his first radio job when he graduated from high school in 1957.

He was the night-man at KORN in his hometown, Mitchell, South Dakota. He remembers playing 45-RPM records on a $19.95 RCA consumer record player. KORN's owner did not want to buy anything more expensive until he was sure that 45's "were here to stay." By that time, they had been on the market for 5 years.

In addition to the usual broadcast related duties, young Sorenson was in charge of "varmint control." The #1 varmint at the time was a mouse that could outmaneuver the fledging radio man.

The announcers, at the time, brought "sack lunches" to work with them. There was a garbage pail next to the control console. It was there the uneaten scraps of the lunches were placed. The troublesome mouse was adept at running up an extension cord and jumping into the wastebasket where he dined on apple cores, banana peels, etc.

Sorenson was tenacious in his efforts to rid the control room of the mouse. Relying on knowledge he'd gained in high school chemistry class, he exterminated the pesky mouse with a dose of carbon tetrachloride, which was used in the control room to clean tape machine heads.

(Most Violent Program in Radio History)

In 1954, 15-year-old Kevin Doran was a high school boy working the Sunday morning shift at WLEA, Hornell, New York. (He bought the station in 1971 and continues to own it at this writing.)

The "Ave Maria Hour" was produced by the Graymoor Friars, outside New York City. Each week, it dramatically told an episode in the life of a saint. The program was delivered to stations on two quarter-hour transcription discs.

Kevin started disc number one and went downstairs to a nearby restaurant for a carryout cup of coffee. In that morning's chapter, a saint was getting a beating when the turntable's needle stuck.

As Kevin made his way up the steps toward his studio, he could hear the beating over the station monitor. When he reached into his pocket for his key, it wasn't there. He retraced his steps, but failed to find it. In desperation, he broke the pain of glass in the studio door. When he reached the turntable, he gently picked up the tone arm—moving it. The beating promptly stopped. The rest of the story was broadcast without incident.

Kevin still remembers those anxious five minutes—still the most frantic of his life. With good Irish humor, he remarks, "Imagine those devout listeners hearing that 5-minute long beating on a Sunday morning—and what about that poor saint?"

(Scared to Death)

Joe Suglia spent more than half his 25-year radio career as a country/western disc jockey in the Kalamazoo, Michigan, market. He not only played the songs, but was also an enthusiastic fan.

On his own initiative (and time), he followed the acts and got interviews with them for his programs. He says, "I met the up and comers, the fading stars, and the "never was stars" at their best and their worst."

He remembers going backstage at a Tanya Tucker concert when she was "on top." She had not shown up. Just minutes before the curtain was to go up, word came that Tanya would not appear. A very nervous young man would have to carry the whole show. He did! The opening act that instantly became the whole show was Garth Brooks.

(Moving Up)

By 1962, he had moved from a sales spot to sales manager to station manager at KGVO in Missoula, Montana. In his lofty new position, he started issuing memos "From the Desk of Earl Morganrouth." They covered almost everything from office procedure to the proper use of toilet paper. One said, "Effective Monday, all employees will wear a white shirt and tie during business hours." Office manager Vonnie Vaught knew he meant announcers and sales people, but he didn't say that. She decided it was "time to bring the newly promoted boss back down to earth." To bruise his ego, on Monday morning, she and the two ladies who worked for her were at their desks, wearing white shirts and ties. Morganrouth quickly made himself clearer verbally by explaining the policy did not include female staffers.

GOING TO THE FAIR

Most small-town managers call it the most challenging time of the year. Dick Billings of KWRT AM/FM, Booneville, Missouri, says it's because, many times, small-town new announcers are recruited from cities where they've had no experience with farms. He tells the story of a young man he hired from Chicago. The station was asked to provide "celebrity contestants" for a cow-milking contest. Dick accompanied his new hire to the barn at the fairgrounds. Once the milking was to begin, Chicago grabbed the cow by its ears. The animal was spooked, dashing about the barn. Dick, raised on a farm, stepped forward and got the animal under control. The young man, under Dick's very careful instruction, milked the cow. "I don't think he won a blue ribbon," Dick says.

In Kentucky, Ted Grizzard had his live microphone on a fairgrounds. Ted told a guest on his program, "I know that farming is hard work for a man, but ma'am tell me about being a farmer's wife." She said, "I do housework, and I can hoe with the best of 'em. I'd say I'm a pretty good 'hoer.'"

(Wrong Person Got the Signal)

Bill Harell is now retired in Kerrville, Texas. For years, he had been manager/co-owner of KVOA/KOYE, Laredo, Texas. County fair time was always a busy time. While the "4-H Livestock Auction" was being broadcast live, Bill hurried to the fairgrounds. He wanted to tell the announcer doing the program to send the broadcast back to the studio for a commercial Bill had just sold. When Bill motioned to the announcer the signal to make the switch, the auctioneer got the idea Bill was signaling the high bid on the reserve champion beef. Unwittingly, Bill had bought it at $3.00 a pound over market price. His daughter, Mrs. Angie Friend, remembers the incident well, saying, "We ate like rich people for the next year."

FROM TV TO RADIO

(It Was A Start)

Back when television stations did a lot of local programming, many people got into radio as an entrée to the more glamorous and better paying TV. Back in the 1950s, Bill Taylor did exactly the opposite. He was working at WLBC-TV, Muncie, Indiana, as an engineer. His duties were restricted to technical things, which he found unsatisfying.

He decided to try his luck at radio and was hired over the phone by John Cashion. Many announcers were hired that way. They were often referred to as "mail order announcers," something like merchandise that was sold by mail order by Sears and Montgomery Ward.

Bill recalls driving up to WGCD at Chester, South Carolina, finding "the boss" with a paper bag next to his chair at the control board. He was conducting a disc jockey show with a lot of adlib comments—many with local flavor. For instance, he was commenting on "the most pregnant woman I've ever seen." He introduced a record saying, "Here's one of those 'gut bucket songs' the kids all like—Pat Boone's record of 'Ain't That A Shame.'"

"When he saw me," Bill remembers, "he called in somebody to finish his show, taking me down to the Moose Club, where he got me drunk. He and I were both at the station the next morning."

John had been "sent down" to Chester by new station owners. John's lack of management experience and his increasing drinking problems made his WGCD career a very short one. When he was fired, he quickly found another job on the air at WORD, Spartanburg, South Carolina. John quickly became a personality of major proportions there. When he died in the 1960s, his funeral was the biggest one in Spartanburg history.

John had given Bill his "chance" in radio, and he made the most of it. Within a few years, he had worked himself up to 50,000-watt WNOE, New Orleans, owned by former governor Jimmy Noe (the father-in-law of Gordon MacLendon). Bill was the sign-on man there.

Noe had bought the station when it was WBNO (Baptists of New Orleans). A condition of the sale was that the Baptist group would continue to have a one-hour program every Sunday morning.

Noe was programming his station along the lines that had made his son-in-law so successful. It was top 40 with a lot of excitement enhanced by a reverberation unit. Whoever had broken in a new Sunday morning part-timer had neglected to tell him how to turn off that unit when the Baptist program came on. That Sunday morning, listeners heard something like "goddddd, saaaaiiidddddd. Yoresee, goooing to helllllll." The reverberation unit was taken out the following day.

The station was on 1060—adjacent to 1050, Mexican station XEG. WNOE was off overnight for transmitter maintenance. On XEG, radio preacher "Brother Al" told his listeners that the best way to fight the devil was to send the brother money.

Bill remembers, with the carrier on, just before he played the "National Anthem," he would turn on the WNOE microphone and announce, "This is the devil. Al is my friend. We split the money. Keep it coming in." Apparently, nobody identified the "devil voice." He was sure enough they would that he stopped the ruse on his own.

(And Another Start)

Most folks in radio get their start as the Sunday morning announcer on a small station. The duties are generally not demanding. You give station breaks and do the openings and closings of mostly paid religious programs.

That's how Jay Braswell got his start. It was at WWNS, Statesboro, Georgia. He still remembers his first Sunday "soloing." He recalls, "I had "patched" the remotes in correctly and played the tapes scheduled without incident. I had given the station breaks and read the program openings and closings flawlessly. I was very proud of myself.

"The last thing on my schedule was reading the closing to the Baptist church service. The preacher this Sunday, as he often did, was running over. At 5 seconds 'til 12, I cut him off, and said into the microphone. 'In Jesus name, Amen. WWNS, Statesboro, Georgia. It's twelve noon.' Again, flawless. Then the telephone rang!

"It was the station manager, who informed me, 'Braswell, you don't need to Amen the damn preacher.'"

(A Pop Guitar Music Background)

For twenty-five years, Larry Long has been one of the "best voices" in the Kalamazoo, Michigan, radio market. He started out during his sophomore year of high school as Sunday announcer at his hometown station, WAOP, Otsego.

In those days, Larry was an aspiring guitar player. He practiced while the taped preachers were on. One Sunday, he forgot to turn off the control room microphone. A couple of preachers had unscheduled pop guitar behind their radio sermons.

(Up Tempo Guy Lombardo)

Charlie Russell of WESR AM/FM, Olney, Virginia, also started his career as a part-timer on Sunday. The owner of a Western Auto Store loved the orchestra and vocalists of Guy Lombardo. He bought 15 minutes of Lombardo music each Sunday afternoon at one-fifteen.

Eighteen-year-old Charlie was not a fan of the "Sweetest Music This Side Of Heaven." He decided it needed pepping up, so he played the 33-1/3 RPM Lombardo records at 45 RPM. Nobody complained, so at least once on each Lombardo program thereafter, there was an "up tempo" speeded-up version of a Lombardo rendition.

(Not In Line for a Pulitzer)

In small radio stations, announcers are often called upon to do non-announcer chores. Sometimes, the results are less than stellar. Example:

The announcer on duty at KERV, Kerville, Texas, had taken an obituary notice over the phone from a local funeral director. When he put it on the air, this is what listeners heard:

> "Karl Smith, age 83, a lifelong resident of this city passed away Tuesday night. Funeral services for Mr. Smith will be held Friday at the First Methodist Church. Entertainment will follow in the church cemetery. Excuse me that should be internment."

Kermit Shafer in
All Time Bloopers (Avenel)

(From the same source)

Sometimes overworked, young announcers in small stations try too hard to sound "big time" with disastrous results. A couple of decades ago, an announcer at KUTY, Palmdale, California, pulled what might be termed "a kuty," reporting: "On the local scene, the shitty sheriff was kept busy last night by two buglers. I mean, 'city sheriff and burglars.'"

TAKE ME OUT TO THE BALLGAME

Baseball games have been on the air since radio's earliest days. Initially, club owners feared that the broadcasts would cut into their crowds. Instead, they learned that the air accounts actually helped attendance by interesting new people in the game and the teams.

Today, in an era of player "free agency," causing rapid turnover of players, the radio broadcasters are the constant that maintains interest and loyalty. With their ranks largely now populated by colorful former players and the current players appearing for interviews, it's compelling entertainment. Some examples from major league broadcasts:

(A Yogism)

After Cincinnati's Johnny Bench broke Yogi Berra's home run record for catchers, Berra told a radio audience, "I thought the record would stand until it was broken."

*

(What's That Score?)

Curt Gowdy, recapping an All Star Game told his audience, "National League 6, American League 4. Once again, American League 6, National League 4."

*

(A Cool One)

Former Yankee pitcher Waite Hoyt was one of the pioneers who made the trip from the playing field to the radio booth. He signed with Burger Brewing Company of Cincinnati to do the Reds games in 1943.

popular baseball announcers ever was Dizzy
major league player. His English got him into
he moved behind the microphone. He was
you know the King's English?" Dizzy replied,
he Queen." And, a very proper gentleman told
really shouldn't say ain't." Dean's reply, "A lot
o don't say ain't—ain't working."

*

(Famous Dizzyism):

re is tied. The runners on first and second are taking
ff their respectable bases. There goes the runner. He
o third base."

t Shafer in
f the Bloopers
el Books)

., from the same source:

ery Minor League Game)

he announcer says, "Here comes the pitch, it's a well-hit
ball. It's going to the straightaway center field. It's going ...
going ... going. It curves foul."

(What?)

Roger Coleman, San Diego "Padres" broadcaster, described a play as follows, "The fast pitch to Tucker Ashford is grounded into left field. No wait a minute. It's low and outside."

*

* = anecdotage.com

The association lasted 24
Hoyt was being sel[e]
and Armed Forc[e]
describing the gam[e]
Then, when it was ti[me]
Network for the pri[ce]
Company, Hoyt ann[ounced]
identification, this is the [...]

For two weeks afterward, [...]
heard about the Gillette pro[...]
Burger ads. Incidentally, Gille[tte]
based Proctor and Gamble.

(Cool, but)

Houston Astros broadcaster Bob Bo[...]
broadcast, "The Astrodome is a toug[h ...]
especially when the air conditioner blows [...]

*

(What A Place to Practice)

Red Barber, one of the all-time great baseball pl[ay]
men, did his first major league game in 1934 whe[n]
hired as sports announcer for the Cincinnati Reds. It [was the]
first major league game he'd ever seen.

In his memoir, Barber says, "That first afternoon at [the]
ballpark I noticed WLW's chief announcer, Peter Grant, wa[s]
sitting quietly beside me." When Grant, without saying
anything, left during the 4th inning, Barber said, "I knew I
was doing it all right."

In the Catbird Seat
With Robert Craemer
(DeCapo Press)

(Dizzy Logic)
One of the mos[t]
Dean, a stellar
trouble when
asked, "Don'[t]
"Sure. So is
Dean, "You
of people w[...]

(The Mo[st]
"The sc[...]
a lead [...]
slud in
Kerm[...]
Best
(Av[...]
An[...]

A LOTTA' LAUGHS

In 2005, Bob Uecker spent his 50th year in professional baseball and his 35th year behind the mike as a Major League Baseball broadcaster. That's only part of Bob's story.

After six years in the big leagues as a catcher (The Braves, Cardinals, Phillies), Uecker left the field and went into the radio booth.

In 1969, he became more than a former major league player and presently a major league sportscaster, Uecker paid a visit to trumpeter Al Hirt's small night spot in New Orleans. Hirt asked him to come onstage. He improvised a short routine of jokes and self-depreciating stories. He was a real hit with the crowd. So much so, that Hirt recommended him for an appearance on the "Tonight" TV show. That led to more than 100 others before Johnny Carson retired in 1992. Uecker also appeared on the Mike Douglas, Merv Griffin and David Letterman shows. He's a one-time host on "Saturday Night Live." He has also appeared in TV sitcoms, movies, and has written a best-selling book, *Catcher in the Wry*.

With six seasons in Major League Baseball and a career long 200 batting average, Uecker's playing career is often the subject of his humor.

(His Career)

"Anybody with ability can play in the big leagues. But to be able to trick people year in and year out like I did, I think is a much greater feat."

(Signing Up)

"I signed with the Milwaukee Braves for $3,000.

"That bothered my dad at the time because he didn't have that kind of dough. But, he eventually scraped it up."

(The Unseen Hero)

"People don't know this, but I helped the Cardinals win the pennant. I came down with hepatitis. The trainer injected me with it."

(Records)

"I set records that will never be equaled. In fact, I hope 90% of them will never be printed."

(Those Records)

"I led the league in 'Get 'em up next time,' and I had slumps that lasted into the winter."

(Arrested)

"One time I got pulled over at 4 AM. I was fined $75.00 for being intoxicated and $400.00 for being with the Phillies."

(Endorsements)

"Sporting goods companies pay me a lot not to endorse their products."

Source: bobuecker.com/quotes

DETOUR BACK TO RADIO HISTORY

The stars of Los Angeles station KMPC in the late 1920s/early 1930s included:

(Related to Everybody in the World)

Cousin Maurice, who always dressed in a morning coat, striped pants and flowing tie arrived at the station telling the personnel, "I'm worth a million, but you can have me for a dime."

He was put on the air at noon, greeting his listeners in five languages, and then telling them, "I'm your Cousin Maurice. I am related to everyone on earth." People were mesmerized by him and briskly bought the products he pitched. They included: a memory course, a red liquid that was to be poured into the bathtub to cure a variety of ailments, an insurance deal called S. O. S. (safety or sorrow).

On all his offers, he gave the station 50% and kept the other half.

Apparently, something from his past caught up with him. He disappeared.

(Soothing the Insomniacs)

Dr. Johnson, with long hair, flowing tie, dark formal suit, was a professor of religion at U.C.L.A.

On KMPC, he soothed his nocturnal audience and offered helpful advice on coping with life. He sold pillow speakers so that his followers could listen to him without disturbing others during after-midnight broadcasts. Like Cousin Maurice, he disappeared.

(The Poet/Philosopher)

Matt Murray called himself the poet and philosopher of the commonplace. He turned out to be a disbarred lawyer.

(Hellfire and Damnation)

Daddy Rango spit into the microphone and "just raised hell." He implored his radio congregation to send money to keep him on the air to "spread the word of God." When the money came in, he pocketed half. The station got the other half.

(Beverly Hillbillies of the Early '30s)

The biggest hit on KMPC was the "Beverly Hillbillies" (a generation before the TV sitcom).

They were genuine backwoods people who lived at Beverly Glen, behind Benedict Canyon. KMPC did not recruit them. They came in off the street.

They developed such a big, loyal following that they soon were spending their off-the-air hours doing personal appearances all over Southern California.

The station's chief announcer, who would go on, not only to bigger things in radio, but would also play many roles in the movies, John McIntire served as the group's interlocutor becoming known as "Mr. Fancy Pants." He became so busy doing appearances with the group that he had to cut back at KMPC.

He and the band appeared in the movie *Hell's Angels*.

Source *The Great American Broadcast* (Dutton)
By Leonard Maltin

(Banned From the Air)

Arch Obler, a premier radio writer, had penned the skit for the CharlieMcCarthy/Edgar Bergan show. It was routinely passed by the NBC sensors who had not considered how it would sound on the air. Mae West was generally believed to be able to say just "hello" and make it sound sexually provocative.

On December 12, 1937, West began reading her dialog with the snake. When the snake got stuck trying to slither through the slats of the fence that protected the forbidden apple tree, she cheered him on with "Oh shake your hips. Ah, you're doin' all right. Get me a big one. I feel like doin' a big apple. Nice goin' swivel hips." She said, "Adam would eat the forbidden fruit like women are goin' to feed men for the rest of time—Applesauce."

The NBC phone bank erupted. A thousand letters of protest were received. They said that the skit was "filthy," "immoral," "obscene." Mae West became an instant persona non grata. The FCC came out strongly against her. It was against policy at NBC to even mention her name on the air.

She was banned. That ban was in effect the rest of her life.

Source: John Dunning in
Encyclopedia of Old-Time Radio
(Oxford Press)

WHAT DO THOSE LETTERS MEAN?

Each radio station has its own exclusive call letters. They are assigned by the Federal Communications Commission. If an owner wishes, he or she can ask for a specific call sign.

All station call letters are four letters long (except those issued in radio's earliest days). Stations east of the Mississippi have call signs beginning with W. Those west of the Mississippi begin with K. There are a few exceptions of stations founded early.

Most often, station call letters are the initials of station founders, or their company, or have a tie-in to the geographic area where the station is located. Some owners like call letters to spell a word that fits the station format.

Here is a sample of intriguing call letters:

ALASKA (Nome) KICY
Descriptive: "Icy"

ARIZONA (Lake Havasu) KBBC
British Broadcasting Company is a tie-in with the London Bridge, which town founder Robert McCullough brought from England. It's the town's most distinctive attraction.

CALIFORNIA (Los Angeles) KJLH
Singer Stevie Wonder named his station, "Kindness, Joy, Love, Hope."

COLORADO (Colorado Springs) KILO
An album rock station. A KILO of what?

CONNECTICUT (Torrington) WSNG
WSiNG. It's a talk station.

GEORGIA (Carrollton) WLBB
The call letters were randomly issued to the station's

founder, Judge Bob Tisinger, who weighed 350 pounds and stood 6 foot 6 inches tall. Someone started the story that WLBB stood for "We Love Butter Beans." The judge joined in the fun, saying the story was true. He held public office in the community for 50 years.

GEORGIA (Brunswick) WMOG
Inspired by poet Sydney Lanier's "Wonderful Marshes of Glynn." Brunswick is in Glynn County.

GEORGIA (Statesboro) WWNS
"Welcome to Where Nature Smiles"

KANSAS (Dodge City) KGNO
For Fun: "Kansas Grows No Oranges"

LOUISIANA (Shreveport) KWKH
Operated early by W.K. Henderson, who is well remembered for his broadcasting to the FRC inspector, "You can kiss my ass. He's tied to the tower in the backyard." Henderson said his call letters stood for "Kill Worry! Keep Healthy."

MASSACHUSETTS (Marshfield) WATD
"We're At The Dump." The station's tower is next to the city dump.

MINNESOTA (Fergus Falls) KGDE (now KBRF)
The founder, pharmacist Charles Jaren, believed his station could "Kill Gloomy Dull Evenings."

PENNSYLVANIA (Indiana) WDAD
A coal town "Where Dollars Are Doubled"

PENNSYLVANIA (Selinsgrove) WYGL
"Wiggle to Work"

Tobacco, by law, has not been advertised on the radio since 1969, but its glories in days gone by are still part of history at these stations:

KENTUCKY (London) WFTG
"Where Fine Tobacco Grows"

KENTUCKY (Maysville)
"World's Finest Tobacco Market"

NORTH CAROLINA (Lumberton) WTSB
"Where Tobacco Sells Best"

VIRGINIA (Danville) WBTM
"World's Best Tobacco Market"

Sometimes, stations get "nicknames" matching their call letters from unfriendly sources:

OHIO (Cincinnati) WLW
"World's Lowest Wages." Probably started by unhappy former employees.

WEST VIRGINIA (Huntington) WSAZ
Station critics no doubt came up with this one: "World's Sorriest Station A to Z."

The builders of WHAM at Rochester, New York, chose it because local industrialist George Eastman thought it sounded nice.

Other call letters and their meanings worth noting:

FLORIDA (St. Petersburg) WSUN
The station was a tourist promotion built by the city government. WSUN equaled "Why Stay Up North."

IOWA (Shenandoah) KMA
Founder Earl May was a big thinker. His station was broadcasted from a town of just 5,000. He said his station was "Keeping Millions Advised."

NORTH CAROLINA (Oxford) WCBQ
A Gospel Station, "We Can't Be Quiet"

PENNSYLVANIA (Philadelphia) WCAU
"Where Cheer Awaits U"

SOUTH CAROLINA (Walhalla) WGOG
"Garden Of the Gods"

It was not a "play" on the call letters, but imagine, the original non-broadcaster owners of pioneer station KGB, San Diego, California, adopted as their station's slogan, "Music for the Sick."

"All Time Best Call Letter Picker"

The award would have to go to Gordon McLendon.

He liked combinations that spelled easy to remember words like: KLIF (Cliff) Dallas, Texas. In Houston, KILT reflected his Scotch ancestry. In Shreveport, he chose KEEL to tie in with the city's shipping industry.

When he went into the San Francisco market with a beautiful music format, he called his station KABL (signifying the city's most famous tourist attraction, the cable car). For his Buffalo, New York, beautiful music station, he chose WYSL (Whistle, which you could do to the music the station played). His all-news station in Chicago was named WNUS (news). His classified ads' station in Los Angeles was christened KADS (ads).

But even McLendon was not infallible. He bought KTSA, San Antonio, Texas, a big military town with a very significant Mexican/American population. He changed the KTSA call letters to KAKI to tie in with the area's military bases. Problem: kaki in Spanish is excrement. McLendon changed the call letters back to KTSA as quickly as was possible.

ECHOES OF BORDER RADIO

It was the most powerful radio station in North America. It broadcast with up to a quarter of a million watts, directional into the United States.

It broadcast hillbilly and western music in the 1930s, '40s, and '50s. In the '50s, the announcer was Paul Kallinger, a native of a small midwestern town who went to radio school after World War II. He went to XERF, mainly, he said, "Because I wanted the thrill of having my voice travel out on such a powerful station."

In a typical week, he received mail from most of the states of the Union and Canada, England, Australia, and Japan.

The station was founded by Dr. John R. Brinkley who got famous and rich transplanting goat glands into humans, restoring aging men's sexual potency. He lost both his Kansas medical license and his U.S. radio station license.

That operation was the focus of part of the Homer and Jethro hillbilly routine in the '50s:

HOMER: "How did the goat surgery go?"

JETHRO: "Not baaaaad."

After Brinkley died in the 1940s, the station was taken over by Mexican interests. It changed hands several times later. In one of those changes of ownership, Paul Kallinger was taken at gunpoint across the Rio Grande. He never went back on the air. He resided in Del Rio the rest of his life.

In the 1960s, the station continued its heavy schedule of paid religious programs, but there was a dramatic change in the music and the host. Wolfman Jack served up rock 'n' roll. The station had been so true to its country music stance that

Kallerman turned down Elvis Presley, a rocker, who offered to do a guest spot on his post-midnight show in the '50s.

Instead of the friendly, smooth Kallerman with his trademark, "Your neighbor along the way," XERF listeners heard, "Who is dis on Wolfman telephone? Speak up! You gotta mind tumor. How sweet are your peaches? Stand on your head and howl!"

Wolfman, like Kallerman, left in what might be called a "hostile takeover."

(High-Powered Salesmanship)

The founder "Dr." Brinkley: "Why are you men holding back? Why do you twist and squirm around that old cocklebar? I'm offering you these low rates and the lifetime guarantee of lifetime service. Come at once to the Brinkley Hospital before it's everlastingly too late."

Another advertiser found it profitable to spend thousands of dollars. He was Dr. Ralph Richards, MsD, PsD, metaphysion, and "friendly voice of the heavens." "Send me the date of your birth and $1.00, and I will search the stars for your future." Thousands upon thousands did.

A seductive, female voice cooed over the air: "Maybe one of you big, strong, handsome men would want to meet me, and maybe spend the rest of your days with me. I am just one of a thousand beautiful, warm, affectionate women who are members of the 'Hollywood 400 Club.'"

The border stations were not the only purveyors of ads of questionable truthfulness for products of doubtful value.

IT MADE YOU FEEL REAL GOOD

In the late 1940s and early 1950s, store shelves were full of it, and radio stations were full of ads for it. The name of the "miracle concoction" was HADACOL. Nothing had caught on like it, in memory.

Bill Mack was on the air on KWFT, Wichita Falls, Texas, for the product for 30 minutes every day. There was a live band with Bill not only announcing, but also singing.

The sponsor's commercials were most often testimonials from satisfied Hadacol users.

Typically, they said, "I have not felt this good since I was young." The most satisfied "Hadacol" customers were older people. They told the radio audience that the "cure all product" was "the greatest thing I've ever found."

"Hadacol" was advertised on U.S. radio stations in large cities and small towns. It favored stations that programmed a lot of what was then known as hillbilly and western music.

The product left the market after it was discovered that it contained a high proportion of alcohol. In Bill's words, "We found out that those people were 'splashed' while they were doing those commercials."

Bill Mack's memoir
From the Trenches of Broadcasting (Unit I)

(Did You Ever See A Bald Sheep?)

Ken Radant, longtime owner-operator of WBCH AM/FM, Hastings, Michigan, remembers another patent medicine that got the big sell on radio in the early 1950s. It was called "Charles Antell Formula Nine." It was a hair product for men containing lanolin. Ken remembers one of the strong selling points in the radio copy was, "Did you ever see a bald sheep?"

(Not A Drop Sold)

In the early 1980s, on over 600 radio stations, listeners heard the praises sung and spoken of a remarkable beverage and the colorful partners in the business that produced it. Their names were "Big Red" and Thor. Their product came in a "flip top" can.

Listeners to the spots enjoyed the company's ball games; songs by their niece, Tanya, an aspiring Nashville star; family Christmas; and finally a fire that put them out of business.

The company's merchandising included copies of their jingles and a book which spelled out "101 Ways" to use it. The jingles "on the Half Moon label" and the book were available at stores everywhere, except in states in which there was a vowel in the state name. The double entendre caused comment but little criticism.

There really wasn't a product. It was a figment of the imagination of disc jockey Terry Dorsey. The make-believe product name was "Hiney Wine." Its slogan was compelling: "You go around only once in life. Grab all the 'Hiney' you can get."

Terry devised the "Hiney Wine" spoof in 1982 at KPLX, Dallas, to cut into its competitor KSCS. It must have worked. KSCS hired Terry in 1988. Syndication was an afterthought.

Terry started as a "rock jock" at WFKY, Frankfort, Kentucky, fresh out of high school. After Viet Nam, he switched to country jocking, first at WHON, Centerville, Indiana, and WONE, Dayton, Ohio, then came to Dallas and "Hiney Wine."

FUN AND GAMES

GET PEOPLE TALKING. You'll get more listeners, and you'll sell more advertising. That's a formula that took hold in the radio business in the 1940s, spread in the 1950s, and soared in the 1960s. The station-sponsored events required people to go find something placed somewhere in the station's listening area.

Gordon McLendon is believed to have used the gimmick first. A certificate for $1,000 (a lot of money in the '50s and '60s) was awarded to the first person who found the treasure. It was not on private property. Clues were broadcast daily helping listeners determine the location of the $1,000.

A Lexington, Kentucky, station that had been the audience and revenue leader for more than half a decade got a new competitor with a "short play list" of the most popular records currently, high profile disc jockeys, jingles, etc., and a $1,000 treasure hunt. The management of the incumbent leader noticed that the females in the office were bringing a sack lunch to work so that they could spend their entire lunch hour searching for the competing station's "treasure."

The longtime leading station changed abruptly to an even shorter play list, still higher-profile disc jockeys, peppier jingles, and more contests with bigger prizes. It held on to its #1 status. But, it was not easy.

(Another Treasure Hunt)

In the Wheeling, West Virginia, market, a day-timer in the suburbs was making a valiant effort to become a contender among the half dozen stations competing there. It launched the market's first "Treasure Hunt."

Dale Tucker broke into radio there. He still remembers his

first day on the job. Ambiguous clues were being broadcast as to the location of the station's "treasure." Over the following month and a half, clues would continue to be broadcast about the hidden $1,000 certificate. The plan was to make the clues more specific, as the contest proceeded. A winner, according to the plan, would find the treasure sometime during the sixth week of the "hunt." Something went terribly wrong for the station!

Two workmen in overhauls came into the station. They'd been "cleaning up" a little park and found the $1,000 certificate. They had not even heard the station, let alone the promotion. They merely found the prize under a picnic table and followed the instructions on it. They brought it to the station.

Behind a closed door, the very young manager, in his first management job, explained he did not have $1,000 in the station checking account, but would have it in six weeks. He swore them to secrecy. New clues continued to be broadcast.

Then, during the sixth week, the two workmen showed up at the radio station. The $1,000 was waiting for them and was awarded to them with much fanfare.

(Not Quite So Lucky)

She had been a U.S.O. entertainer during World War II. After hostilities ended, she went to Lexington, Kentucky, where she was hired to conduct a daily half-hour women's program on WKLX (now WLXG). The vivacious Ms. Frances Knight was popular on the air, but she thought she could be even more popular if she conducted a contest on it. She was a "big thinker."

In cooperation with a furniture store that advertised on her program, she announced, "I'm going to give away a whole house full of furniture." Nothing like that had ever been done in the '40s small city of 50,000.

On each day's program, Ms. Knight would pose a "question of the day." Listeners were asked to phone in their answers within five minutes. Each day, when a question was not answered, a prize was added. It started in mid-October, and Ms. Knight hoped by Christmas the prizes added, one a day, would equal a whole house full of furnishings. Questions were very tough initially, getting easier as Christmas neared.

On December 12, the question was very, very tough—the kind of question nobody could answer in 5 minutes, but a miracle happened. A listener called in with the correct answer.

When someone wins a big prize, the host or hostess would be expected to enthusiastically holler "Congratulations!" As Ted Grizzard tells it in his memoir, *#1 is Chicken*, there was silence for at least five seconds, then the charming radio hostess with a genuine touch of disgust in her voice said, "I could just kill you. You've ruined my program. I didn't want a winner until Christmas."

(Trying Too Hard)

It was Lou Vito's first Christmas running his own stations, WPKO/WBLL, Bellefontaine, Ohio in 1988.

On the Saturday morning after Thanksgiving, Lou had leased the downtown theatre. He announced that while parents were shopping, they could drop their children off for "Free Cartoons." The idea had done well in other towns during earlier Christmas seasons.

Just "doing well" was not enough for Lou. He wanted the promotion to give his newly acquired stations a "real jolt." A live Santa Claus was brought in. To add more zest to the promotion, radio friend Terry Kah also brought in a live monkey. In Lou's words, "Everything went wrong."

First, the little monkey fell off his trapeze. Lou's staffers,

Dan Weldy and Jim Stoner, had to chase the monkey before he did serious damage to one of the children and the stations' reputation.

Second, the weather was unseasonably warm in Northern Ohio. The temperature was in the low 80s. Instead of talking to the kiddies, the hired Santa was hiding out in a cool spot. Lou told him to "get ready to sweat a little and begin taking the kids' orders for Christmas toys."

Chaos had broken out in the theatre. To restore order, Lou told staffer Jim Stoner, a music major in college, to lead an unplanned Christmas sing-a-long. With the singing of the familiar Christmas songs and carols, order was restored and the promotion turned out to be successful. It was a success that Lou never tried to repeat.

(Buried Alive)

Don Martin was a very big thinker in a very small place. Salem, Indiana, where his daytime-only radio station WSLM is located, had a population of about 4,000 people back in the '60s. WSLM listeners were woken each morning by the sound of a braying donkey. Martin says, "No other station did that."

Don found out that the record for a person living underground constantly was 66 days. With help from others at the station, a compartment was built, and a hole was dug in Salem's downtown business district.

Don recruited a local unemployed man to go underground and stay there until he beat the world record—if possible.

Don nicknamed his record seeker "Mike the Mole."

Advertising was sold on frequent reports. Afterwards, Don said, "We broke the record. He was down there 66½ days and was the subject of a lot of news stories over a wide area of the country. It really caused a lot of talk, but, I think, we lost money. City officials demanded that we post someone near the 'mole's' underground living quarters, while he was down there. That cost us a lot of money."

(It's a Bird! It's a Plane! It's a Bird!)

Paul Howard of West Virginia Radio remembers, in the late 1950s, WCAW 680 on the dial at Charleston, West Virginia, was on the top floor of the Kanawha Hotel. The station adopted a mascot, a live black crow. The crow was kept in a cage in the control room. The cage measured 7 feet long, 4 feet wide, and 4 feet high. He was nicknamed "Matey from Six-eighty."

The station's elderly janitor was deathly afraid of the bird, so the morning man was assigned the task of rolling the paper out of the cage each morning to dispose of the bird's droppings.

One of the jocks, Cliff Tobey, took a particular fancy to the "pet." He let him out of the cage during his program. The bird walked around the studio. Cliff talked to him on the air. Manager Pete Johnson was not a fan of the conversations between Tobey and "Matey." The live bird was replaced by a plastic one; a 3-foot crow decked out in a tux. It had been made to advertise "Old Crow Whiskey." Because of the broadcaster's self-imposed ban on hard liquor advertising on the air, the origin of "Matey's" plastic replacement was never divulged on WCAW.

(Wrong Message)

Hal Widson, who manages KWED at Seguin, Texas, 40 miles east of San Antonio, was formerly manager of an FM station in the city. One of his competitors there was KISS.

He remembers, they worked hard and smart for two years to

let the business community know that their audience was upscale young men wearing three-piece suits and driving sports cars. The conservative business community was increasingly buying into the new image KISS was selling, and then there was a major drug bust in the city. It was so big that it got a front-page story in the local daily newspaper, plus a big picture of the "drug kingpin" being arrested. He was wearing a KISS t-shirt.

(Due to Circumstances Beyond Our Control)

Between Christmas and New Year's used to be a very slow time for advertising. Someone thought up the idea of pepping things up by honoring "The First Baby of the Year."

The promotion ran successfully for several years on one station, and then things began to change. The father of the "first baby" picked up certificates for 15 prizes from 15 local businesses. He was very appreciative to each of them and made a couple of purchases, for which he paid by check. Problem was the checks were for insufficient funds, "cold."

The station and the 15 advertisers agreed that sometimes things don't work out as planned. They staged the same promotion the next holiday season. Another problem: the mother and father of the "First Baby of the Year" were unwed and made no bones about it, but they insisted on being declared the winner on the air and getting the prizes. Then radio station management and the 15 sponsors unanimously agreed that the promotion had been made obsolete by a change of "social mores."

(Second Honeymoon?)

In the south, it's a big powerful station in a town where everybody knows everybody else. The station sponsored a "sign up to win" contest. Promotional announcements invited listeners to register to win a Caribbean cruise. The announcements suggested it would be a perfect win for honeymooners or second honeymooners.

The winners that the station and advertisers thought were ideal were a couple, around 50 years old. When they boarded, the husband was dazzled by an unescorted female he met in the bar. When the boat stopped "at a port of call" for shopping and sightseeing, the wife boarded a plane for home. Once there, she went to a lawyer's office and filed for divorce.

(Subject to Change)

Laurie Prax, co-owner/operator of KVAK AM/FM, Valdese, Alaska, says, "Living on the coast of Alaska has its challenges. When you plan outdoor events, you have to stay flexible."

As an example, she says, "When snow changed to rain during our annual "Snow Sculpture Contest," the on-air talent quickly made the decision to change "Snow Park" into "Slush Park." Features were a toboggan ride for kids and a human slip-slide made out of heavy duty plastic. Children and adults of all ages enjoyed it. We didn't let it rain on our parade, or I should say, event."

(Bad Luck in 2s)

Mark Allen has been a practicing attorney. For over a decade, he has been the association executive of the Washington State Broadcasters Association. Before that, he was a radio personality on some of the west coast's best radio stations. Thirty years ago, he was on KSJO, San Jose, California. He remembers:

It was ratings time, and KSJO decided to make a "big splash." "We announced that we would be giving away a brand new car that month. We started the announcements on the air, even though the manager had not made an advertising trade for the car. Without the car, we started broadcasting scrambled clues. The listener who solved the clues would get the car. Finally, half way through the first week of the contest, we got the car. It was a brand new 'Vega' and our listeners were excited."

Mark continues, "We were broadcasting a sentence with one word absent. The winner was to pick that word. We did not believe it was an easily solved contest, but, believe it or not, on Saturday night at 11:30, the winning guess came in less than six days after the contest started. We had over three weeks to go in the rating period and nothing to give away.

"We were surprised and happy to find out that our owner was very understanding," Mark adds. "He gave us a thousand dollars to give away—a lot of money in the early 1970s."

He goes on to say, "We obtained a safe with a combination lock on it. We had obtained a $1,000 certificate of deposit at a local bank. The deposit was put in the safe.

"We planned to take our safe to various locations where people would try their luck at dialing the 'winning combination.' We sent our evening disc jockey to a local high school football game. At halftime, a cheerleader was to take a crack at opening the safe. She twiddled the dial, and unbelievably, it unlocked the safe. When the door opened, the cheerleader reached inside and was a thousand dollars richer. This time, we were out of the prize business for the duration of the rating period—over two more weeks."

(It Wasn't A Real Radio Station)

In *TV Guide's Guide to TV* (Barnes and Noble Books), "WKRP in Cincinnati" is described as "Hugh Wilson's ensemble driven, three-time Emmy nominee, tuned to the antics of a radio station where an innovative program director and his wacky colleagues set out to change the station format from easy listening to rock 'n' roll." The witty series had many fans, but the CBS Network kept changing its time. Finding the program was not an easy matter. Its first network run ran from September 1978 through September 1982. A revamped series titled "The New WKRP" ran in syndication from 1991 to 1993.

One of the most memorable episodes was a pre-Thanksgiving yarn about an ill-fated promotion in which turkeys were dropped from an airplane prior to that holiday. WKRP and its staff were all fictional, but the turkey-dropping incident was apparently based on fact.

(The Real Story)

When David Luther, now the administrator of the "International Radio Idea Bank," went to work as group program director of Steve Bellinger's Illinois radio station group in the mid '60s, Bellinger told him this story, over a decade before the TV episode on "WKRP" aired:

"For Thanksgiving, I bought a big, beautiful turkey to be given away at WDZ at Decatur. I recorded 'promos' telling people to be at our local shopping center on Monday morning (before Thanksgiving). 'Look up in the sky for my plane,' I told them. 'Someone is going to win the biggest, most beautiful Thanksgiving turkey in town, and there's a fifty-dollar bill attached to each turkey leg. That's a turkey and one-hundred dollars in cash.'"

Steve goes on, "On the appointed morning, I got into the plane with the turkey by my side. I flew over the shopping center several times, then I let loose the turkey. I hollered 'Fly, damn you, fly.' The turkey crashed down onto the roof of a clothing store in the center. When the crowd saw what had happened, there was a loud scream. As I looked down, I decided I had better not land at the local airport. I went fifty miles to another airport where I hoped no one had heard about the 'turkey disaster' in Decatur. They had."

For the next several days, there was a lot of angry mail received at the station. Some people threatened to have Bellinger arrested for cruelty to a bird. They didn't.

Afterwards, Bellinger said, "I wish somebody had told me domesticated turkeys can't fly. Wild turkeys can fly." He added thoughtfully, "Who'd want to eat a wild turkey anyway?"

(Go To Hell)

WMIR, the little day-timer at Lake Geneva, Wisconsin (population 7,599), set the town "on its ear" when it told listeners to sign up for a trip to Hell on Halloween. They weren't kidding. Hell is a small, unincorporated community in southeast Michigan, about twenty miles from Ann Arbor. The prize would include dinner at a place called, "The Devil's Den."

Hell has a non-accredited university, which issues signed diplomas. It has a post office in back of its general store. It has a local bar called "The Dam Site." The winning couple told the station on returning from their trip, "We had a hell of a good time."

Valarie Geller in
Powerful Radio (M Street)

(WMIR is now owned by a religious broadcaster out of Green Bay, Wisconsin. WLKG, an FM station, has taken over as the town's community station.)

RADIO "Q" AND "A"

1. At the end of Orson Wells' unforgettable "Mercury Theatre" version of "The War of the Worlds," how were the Martians defeated?

2. What was special about the date of Arthur Godfrey's last radio series broadcast: the April 30, 1972 edition of "Arthur Godfrey Time"?

3. When Don McNeil's "Breakfast Club" went off the air in 1968, how long had McNeil hosted the show?

4. What brought Chicago-based Paul Harvey to national attention soon after he began his long running news program to ABC?

5. What was the last record played on WABC, New York, on May 10, 1982, when the long running "Top 40" behemoth changed to all-talk programming?

(Answers are on the next page.)

From *505 Radio Questions*
Harry Castleman and
Walter J. Operatic (Walker and Co.)

Answers to RADIO "Q" AND "A"

1. They were destroyed by common earth bacteria against which they had developed no built-in resistance.

2. It marked 27 years to the day of Godfrey's first broadcast of "Arthur Godfrey Time" for the network on April 30, 1945. It also marked the end of the variety-show format on the CBS Radio Network.

3. Thirty-five years and six months before, Don McNeil had started with the "Pepper Pot" Program on the NBC Blue Network on June 23, 1933. Staying with the show, as it changed its name to "The Breakfast Club," that title remained even after the network had changed its name from the Blue Network to the ABC. On December 27, 1968, the series ended.

4. Paul Harvey was arrested on February 6, 1951, for sneaking into the Aragonne Atomic Lab in Lamont, Illinois, to demonstrate the lab's lax security. He was brought before a grand jury, but no indictments resulted. Harvey's national radio program had started three months before on December 31, 1950. It was only on Sunday nights on ABC.

5. John Lennon's "Imagine." This was the last rock song played on New York's main rock outlet for twenty years.

GO FOOTBALL! GO!

Though the season is short, compared to baseball or basketball, football is big, very big, all across the country—high school, college, the pros.

It attracts a big, very vocal audience everywhere and is "home" to some of sports most colorful men on the field and in the broadcast booth.

(Where?)

"And, he's got an icepack on his groin there, so, it possibly is not the old shoulder injury."

Sportscaster Ray French
Frontiernet

(Colorful Description)

WCVL (Crawfordsville, Indiana) was covering the Purdue-Northwestern game. LeRoy Keys was Purdue's fast running back. The sportscaster enthusiastically told the radio audience that Keys "Purdue's fastest running black (INSTEAD OF BACK) is expected to be key to the 'Boilermaker' showing today."

(Not What They Used To Be)

In Pro Football, the "Green Bay Packers," after the glorious days under Vince Lombardi, was having a down season. The radio sportscaster lamented, "It's not the shame team that it once was. Green Bay beat the bust again today." (*SHAME* SHOULD HAVE BEEN *SAME*—*BUST* SHOULD HAVE BEEN *DUST*.)

(Out of His Element)

He was a very good sportscaster, but at all small stations like

WSIP, Paintsville, Kentucky, staffers have to do more than one job. In addition to calling games, this particular sports announcer also hosted an hour-long, easy-listening music program.

The young man, who knew little about easy music or cared much about it, sometimes "snuck in a top-40 number." On one program, he was heard to say, "Here's one of the more popular records from the Top-40 chort." (INSTEAD OF *CHART*)

(Unusual Game Interruption)

The football announcer told his audience, "Many different kinds of animals have interrupted football games, but none so unusual as the one today. It's a big hippity-hop rabbit, jacking off down the field."

(A Great Opening Drive)

Calling the play-by-play of the high school football game at WBYE, Calera, Alabama, was indeed exciting. The home team had taken the opening kickoff and had ground out hard-won yardage. Recapping the drive, the announcer ended with this declaration, "For the first time in the game, the 'Warriors' have their balls in their hands...er ah...I mean their hands on the ball."

Kermit Schafer in
Prize Bloopers (Avenel)

(The Worst Way)

"Jack has a bad knee, but limps back into the huddle. He wants to play this game in the worst way...and that's what he's doing," the high school football announcer opines.

(Old Pro That He Is)

New York Giants' radio announcer: "Ken Strong of our

Giants, old pro that he is, calmly stepped back and kicked a 49-year-old field goal."

Kermit Schafer
Prize Bloopers (Fawcett)

(Whichever Comes First)

Ahead of the season, a sports announcer of the New Orleans Saints was interviewing a Saints' running back. He asked him if he had goals for the new season. He answered, "I want to rush for a thousand or fifteen hundred yards—whichever comes first."

(The Best)

An NFL "Hall of Famer" told a radio interviewer calmly, "I feel like I'm the best, but you're not going to get me to say that."

(The Most Famous Football Fluff of All)

"He has the ball on the ten, the twenty, the thirty, the forty. Look at that 'son of a bitch' run."

(Challenge)

Denny Cooley called high school football for twenty years. "Looking back," he says, "many times getting the games on the air was a bigger challenge than doing the broadcasts."

He remembers driving three hundred miles to cover a regional championship football game in Cheboygan. An afternoon snowstorm had dropped a dozen inches of snow in just a matter of hours. All of the highway department and commercial snow removal equipment was busy opening the roads. When he and his fellow sportscaster, Terry Bonnel, arrived at the playing field, there were over fifty snow blowers that football fans had brought from home to clear away the snow for the game on WQXCI, Ostego, Michigan.

(Colorful)

Archie Morgan, owner of WIXE, Monroe, North Carolina, remembers well his start in radio. It hasn't been that long ago. It was in 1988.

One of the best stories he tells, on himself, was after just two months in the business, his boss asked him to do color on the local football broadcast. He showed up early, checked through to the station, and was as ready as a man of very light experience could be.

"The coach of the opposing team, a friend of my boss, came by to invite us to join him for something to eat before the game. We enjoyed large meatball subs.

"About six minutes into the broadcast, my boss during a cut-away to the station told me, 'I'm sick. You'll have to fill in for me 'til I get back.'

"When play resumed, I did my best. The opposing team's running back was a great player. He got the ball on almost every play. I didn't know his name. He was black. I said something like, 'That big, black, colored kid has the ball again and he takes it up the middle for a big gain.'

"It seemed like an eternity, but the boss got back and took over the play-by-play again. When I told him about my description during his absence, he said, "You brought new meaning to 'color man.'"

(Who's That?)

Bill Harell remembers his early outings as a high school football radio play-by play man. He remembers one night on KVOP, Plainview, Texas. He was doing the starting lineups for the visiting team. He hadn't looked them over ahead of time. He was stopped cold reading that the visiting team's starting quarterback would be Jesus??? He gulped, then spelled the name. He soon found out that Jesus (pronounced "HAY-SOOS") is a common name in Mexican-American communities.

(Talk About Action)

At KSEN, Shelby, Montana, the home team was "on the road." It was homecoming night for the host school. Jerry Black, owner-manager, was broadcasting the game. At halftime, a large group of people crowded around the public address system for homecoming ceremonies. KSEN was right next to that "P.A."

While he was recapping the first-half action on the radio, Black kept moving back for the people doing the ceremony. In the confusion, he backed off the platform, dropping about ten feet, microphone in hand. Radio listeners heard a distant voice saying, "We'll be back after this message from the studio."

History of Montana Broadcasting
C. Howard McDonald (Big M)

(Where Are We?)

Heard on a small college radio broadcast in the Midwest: "Good afternoon. It's a beautiful day for football here in??? Where the hell are we?"

IN THE PUBLIC INTEREST

Since 1927, first, the Federal Radio Commission (FRC), and later, beginning in 1935, the Federal Communications Commission (FCC) have mandated that radio stations are to "serve the public interest, convenience, and necessity." One of the principal ways that stations do that is broadcasting announcements concerning topics of concern to the people in their listening areas. Sometimes, the messages don't come over the air as intended. This may have been caused by a careless copywriter or an announcer's mistake or "fluff." We do not point blame here. But, merely report some of the human foibles that appeared on the radio as a station put forth its best effort to keep its promise to its licensor and its listening public.

(Lost and Found)

On a New England station, the following was heard:

"When you're lost in the deep woods, don't panic. Just drop a postcard to the Forest Department, Box 833, Burlington, Vermont. You'll be sent a free booklet with sound advice in such situations."

(Children?)

"At this event, children must be accompanied by an adult under 12 years of age."

(Drive Safely)

"Motorists, when you get behind the wheel, be sure to keep a safe distance from the car in front of you. Tail-getting will get you nowhere. That should be tail-gating."

(In the Swim of Things)

"The American Red Cross sends you this life-saving tip: In case of drowning, lay the girl...lay the drowning victim on her back and try mouth-to-mouth breeding—breathing."

(Call a Girl)

The following was heard on a small station in the Northeast: "If you need assistance with your call, call 222-3123. A cheerful call girl will be at your service."

(Free of Charge)

"Don't forget, the X-Ray Unit will examine you for tuberculosis and other diseases, which you will receive free of charge."

(Nurse!)

"Young lady, your country needs you. Hospitals throughout the country are understaffed. Nurses are urgently needed. Sign up to be one of America's white-clapped angels of mercy." *CLAPPED* SHOULD HAVE BEEN *CAPPED*.

(Help Wanted)

"Your local police department is looking for young, aggressive men to serve a life in law enforcement. New recruits will be given extensive training in handling of firearms, marksmanship, and finger-painting."

(Time Check)

"It's ten-thirty in Chicago. Do you know where your parents are?"

(Good Spirits)

"The First Methodist Church Bazaar Committee announces that there will be plenty of booze for sale. I mean, there will be plenty of booths for sale."

(Hunting Misfortune)

"The State Conservation Department is sorry to announce this distressing news. Since the hunting season officially opened, eight deer hunters have been shot in the hunting area designated for deer hunting. All of them were mistaken for deer wearing red jackets."

(Don't Miss It)

"This Sunday, Reverend R.J. Ryan will speak 'In Spite Of Everything.'"

(Tough One to Announce)

"Listeners in this area are invited to an Open House at the Fire Station next to Town Hall. See twelve ambulances and twelve firetwucks—that's trewlve twucks."

(Special Election)

"Vote in tomorrow's special election on zoning and package liquor stores. You free loaders, I mean free holders, be sure to vote."

BEYOND THE CALL OF DUTY

Normally, radio stations don't limit their public service activities to just brief announcements.

Often, they go out of their way to do something very special to address a problem in their communities. Here are a couple of examples:

(Music to Drive to the Dump By)

It was the brainchild of Ken Squire, whose family has owned WDEV, Waterbury, Vermont, since its beginning in 1931.

Squire, like other people who make their homes in the area, is very concerned about keeping it neat and clean.

The Saturday morning 8:45 program is a gentle reminder that it's time to make a trip to the dump, and WDEV wants to make it an enjoyable experience with "Music to Drive to the Dump By."

(Fired Up)

In 1961, Bill Willis, longtime owner/operator of WFLQ, French Lick, Indiana, was the chief engineer of WARL/WAVA, Arlington, Virginia, in the Washington, D.C., suburbs.

Inspectors from the FCC made frequent rules compliance visits to radio stations. On the list of rules they checked was one that said that the area around a station's tower had to be kept free of high weeds. That was one of the regular duties of the "chief."

During mid-afternoon, Willis called the local fire department advising them that he was about to burn the weeds around the station tower. They gave him their okay.

The station had a water hose that reached from the side of the studio building all the way out to the tower. Willis strung it out, just in case the unforeseen happened.

He got his fire going. Then, without warning, a gust of wind came up, spreading the fire. It struck the "emergency hose," breaking it in two and making it inoperative.

The sudden fire was reported, and fire trucks with sirens blazing arrived. The fire was extinguished. Those sirens could be plainly heard over the air, where newsman Don Owens was conducting a live public service program. His guest? The local fire chief. The topic? Guarding against grass and weed fires.

(I'll Drink To That)

Disc Jockey Todd Baker at KLYK, Longview, Washington, became intoxicated on the air. Under the supervision of the Washington State Patrol, he was given breath tests every 15 minutes.

After an hour and a half of imbibing a drink of "Jack Daniels" every 15 minutes, he was too drunk to operate the control board. By the end of his four-hour show, he had consumed an entire bottle.

The Patrol had to take him home. In his drunken confusion, he flipped on the patrol vehicle's flashing blue light.

A WORD FROM OUR SPONSOR

Back when I first started selling radio advertising, most of the commercials were read live. On the small stations where I worked in those days, the folks on the air were "pretty green" and learned their craft by the best, but generally the most painful educational system, experience. That means, we made a lot of mistakes.

I think the most valuable ability that I polished during those early days was being able to tell a customer "I'm sorry" like I meant it. I did.

Most commercials on the radio are now recorded. The technology that has developed over the years in the radio business has not only brought efficiency, it has brought about "quality control," which any business must offer its customers and, in the radio business, its listening audience.

For those who "pine for the good old days," it's good to go back in time and listen to some of the commercial "bloopers" that were actually heard on the nation's stations. They were collected by the late Kermit Schafer and distributed in books, on records, and even in a movie. The books are still available on book sites on the World Wide Web, particularly in their selection of out-of-print and used books like: *Pardon My Blooper*, *Prize Bloopers*, *Best of Bloopers*, *Super Duper Bloopers*, *All Time Bloopers*, and in the 380-page *Bloopers, Bloopers, Blooperes*. Out of the thousands of funny commercial bloopers (funny now, but not at the time), we bring you these:

(I Remember Mama)

"Give the lovely Cannon Towel set to either your sister, your aunt, niece, or mother as a wedding present."

(It's A Great Life)

"So go to your neighborhood theatre and see this thrilling new movie. It's a story of passion...bloodshed...lust and death...in fact everything that makes life worth living."

(Try Peanuts)

"So friends, be sure to visit Frankie's Fine Restaurant for elephant food and dining. The portions may be elephant size, but I meant to say elegant size."

(Out of Tune)

On WLOA, Braddock, Pennsylvania, "Remember, this is the highest priced, low quality piano on the market."

(A Big Pipeline)

"Our 'Want Ads' of the air continue with this opportunity: Wanted 100 men to lay Virginia...pipe."

(Nice Trick If You Can Do It)

"If you want to learn how to write, write us for free lessons."

(Screwed Up)

"So try the new Hammer Beverages with a new screwy cap—I mean screw on cap."

(Working Up an Appetite)

"Mama Mia's Pizza really cares about your pizza. None of her pizzas are ever prefrozen. All Mama's pizzas are made to order while you mate—wait."

(Liver Boy)

He was one of the nation's top morning disc jockeys, but he

did "bloop" once in awhile. Bob Steele of WTIC, Hartford, Connecticut, one morning told his listeners, "Two families can liver...uh, love better than one...live better than one."

(That's Quite a Difference)

"So, ladies take advantage of the Elizabeth Arden special offer at Jordon Marsh Stores, where you'll get V.D. at no extra charge...of course I mean, Visible Difference."

(Don't Bug Me)

"Your home deserves a monthly termite inspection. When you think of pests, think of Chuck O'Hara, your Terminex man."

(A Fish Story)

A North Carolina restaurant, City Shellfish, will never be the same since the local announcer read their commercial thusly, "So come in to the Shitty Selfish, I mean silly shitfish...oh hell, let's go back to the news."

(Occasional Pieces)

A longtime announcer on WBAT, Marion, Indiana, fell victim to a copywriter's mistake and came out with the following, "Reiger's Furniture Store features the finest, most durable furniture available. Shop at Reiger's where we've been servicing the housewife for twenty-six years."

(Let's Make a Deal)

"Friends and neighbors, we have such a wide selection of new and used cars that we want you to come down right now and make a deal. Bring your wife along. We can dicker."

(A Hot Number)

"So, stop by our downtown store and visit our fashion center.

You'll see our lovely models in heat—PAUSE AS HE TURNS PAGE—resistant fabrics, which will keep you cool all summer."

(At a Loss for the Right Words)

"So remember folks, we have all the latest models in hard tops and convertibles at prices you can't afford to miss. Yes, folks at Courtesy Motors, your loss is our gain."

(It's a Business Doing Pleasure With You)

"Ladies who care to drop off their clothes will receive prompt attention."

(Fit To Be Tongue-Tied)

"So girls, come on down for the twenty-five percent off sale on all Playtex bras. Be sure to take advantage of this money-saving sale. Playtex will really give you the correct tit…oh, excuse me, that's fit."

If you're on the air live, I'll bet you're glad that Kermit Schafer and his band of "blooper scoopers" are not covering the country and its radio stations now.

(What Did He Say?)

Back in the '70s, most ads on WGOH, Grayson, Kentucky, were recorded like at most stations, but Francis Nash says, there was one local advertiser who insisted his ads be read live. He ran 6 every Friday. The name of the business was Stidham's Shoe Store. Nash says, "Everybody at the station, including me, got a chance at embarrassing himself saying Stidham's Shoe Store."

(On the Air Diagnosis)

Skeeter Dodd remembers Slim Martin at WPET, Goldsboro,

North Carolina, winding up a message for A.K.P. Furniture and Appliance saying, "And don't forget their great service and repair department. If it won't work, take it to Karl and Paul. If they can't fix it, there's something wrong with it."

(Wrong Song)

The new programmer at WRDS, Charleston, West Virginia, had instituted a "back announce policy." Names of the artists and song titles were to be announced after a record had played. Dewey Caldwell had given his all in delivering a Joe Holland Chevrolet Used Cars commercial, telling listeners, "Every car is priced to sell this weekend at Joe Holland Chevrolet." He then hit the following record cold, "I Wouldn't Buy A Used Car from That Man" by Pretty Norma Jean.

(A Sign Painter With Balls)

At WFHG, Bristol, Virginia, "The Sammy Kaye Sunday Serenade" was sponsored by a local sign company, Tickle Brothers. When announcer Rex Rainey closed the program, he told his listeners, "Remember friends, before you buy any sign, test Tickle's."

RADIO ANNOUNCER TEST

During radio's "golden age" from roughly 1928 until the arrival of television in the late 1940s, aspiring radio announcers were asked to take a test, like the one that follows, before being considered.

Try it! See how well you do:

Penelope Cholmondely raised her azure eyes from the crabbed scenario. She meandered along the congeries of her memoirs. There was kenetic algernon, a choleric artificer of icons and triptychs who wanted to write a trilogy. For years she had stifled her risibilities with dour moods. His asthma caused him to sigh like the zephyrs among the Tamarack.

From *Raised on Radio*
Gerald Nachman
(Pantheon)

How did you do?

SELLING RADIO ADVERTISING

(A Blemish on Their Records)

Don Shetley and Carlisle Henderson are longtime residents of Union, South Carolina. They are churchgoers and active in their community. All their lives, they've been men of good reputation.

The two of them were salespeople at the local radio station (WBCU) back in the 1950s. Their pursuit of an advertising business took them one day to the small community of Whitmire, just south of the Union county line.

They spent a profitable day in Whitmire, signing up several of the local merchants to advertise a "sign up to win" promotion in which the lucky winners would get a free winter vacation trip.

Their first day in Whitmire was so successful that they returned the following day.

That day, they were met by a town policeman who asked them to show him their "solicitor's license." Shetley quickly responded by getting out his billfold and showing the policeman his FCC Radio Engineering License. He was informed, quickly, that was not satisfactory, and he and Henderson were taken to the city jail in the town's lone police cruiser. They were put in a jail cell. There was no lock on the door.

They were reloaded into the police cruiser and taken down into the town's "flats" where they would appear in front of the mayor/city judge. He held court in his little restaurant.

As "his honor" started the trial, he was interrupted several times by customers ordering hamburgers and soft drinks, the restaurant's bill of fare. A couple of times the trial was interrupted when a customer came up to claim a "payoff" on illegal vending machines in the restaurant.

The Whitmire city attorney "got wind" of the trial and hurried down. The two radio salesmen had called back to Union to get help from the station's attorney. The two lawyers agreed that the city ordinance under which the salesmen had been arrested was a flawed one. The proceedings quickly ended.

That city ordinance had been drawn up by the owner of the only advertising medium in Whitmire, the weekly newspaper. He had persuaded his fellow city councilmen to pass it.

Ironically, forty years later, Whitmire had suffered the fate of many little towns. Its business district had pretty much "dried up." The newspaper owner had died. A new owner, a local person, had taken the struggling publication over. Mike Stevens, a several-times employee of WBCU, was also a minister of music. He was hired by the First Baptist Church at Whitmire. When he and his wife saw the local newspaper, they could tell it was in trouble. When they approached the lady who was its owner about burying it, she said, "It's not worth anything. If you want it, I'll give it to you." They took it.

(Salesperson Recruiting)

In 1979, Dean Sorenson was building his chain of small-town radio stations in the Upper Midwest. That venture would ultimately make him very rich and well known in broadcasting circles from coast to coast.

When he purchased KOBH in isolated Hot Springs, South Dakota, he promoted a salesperson at KWAT, Watertown,

South Dakota, to manager of the newly acquired venture.

In Dean's words, Doug Olson "got hold of the station quickly and became a part of the community. He and I agreed, he needed a fulltime salesman to further improve the station's fortunes."

An older man named Tommy showed up in Hot Springs looking for a job. Doug was not willing to hire him on his own. He asked for help in evaluating the prospect from Dean and also Jim Thompson, his right-hand man in sales. Tommy was given bus fare and sent to Pierre, then Sorenson's headquarters.

Dean remembers, "Tommy called from the bus station when he arrived. I told him I'd meet him in a café nearby. When I arrived, I had no trouble picking him out of the crowd. He was obviously an old radio guy who was down on his luck."

Dean took Tommy to his office for a formal interview. Thompson told Dean, "I'll just sit in the corner and observe, if that's alright with you."

Dean was asking some probing questions to find out what his prospect's "baggage" was. Tommy admitted that he had had a drinking problem. He had been through treatment.

"Are you in a maintenance program?" Dean asked. He replied, "No, but I've got the numbers." When Dean inquired about the numbers, Tommy told him that he had phone numbers in case he needed support and assistance in a moment of weakness.

Tommy then wiggled a little in his chair and from his right pants pocket a pint bottle of vodka plunged to the floor. He was still quick thinking. Without hesitation, he reached down and swooped up the bottle, putting it inside the breast pocket of his jacket explaining, "I carry this around to remind me of the old days."

Dean had no more questions for Tommy. For Jim, he had one, "When does the next bus leave town?"

(Consultants)

Over the years, radio station managements have kept hundreds of sales consultants busy. None is more fondly remembered by the "old timers" than the late Eddie Algood of Danville, Virginia. He traveled the country for Radio Advertising Bureau between jobs at WBTM and WDVA. He was flamboyant, but his advice was very straightforward. He told salespeople in his audiences, "If there's a problem with an account, go see him quickly. By tomorrow, that problem could be twins."

(Listen)

The late Jim Kokash who managed KHAS, Hastings, Nebraska, for years, told his salespeople, "God gave you two ears—just one mouth. He obviously intended for you to listen more, talk less."

(Worst First Call)

Wandell Allegood of KSLO/KOGM, Opelousas, Louisiana, is the dean of the radio people in his area. He's seen a lot come and a lot go. He remembers one young fellow who made the "worst call" anyone has ever made.

He had been hired as a salesman for one of Wandell's neighbors, the station at Crowley. His shirt was well ironed. His tie was in a neat Windsor knot. His shoes were polished, suit freshly cleaned.

He looked like a salesman, but was he a salesman?

He was about to make the first call on the first day of his new career.

He opened the door of a drugstore. Reluctantly, he stepped inside. Behind the prescription counter was a man in a white coat, the store's pharmacist and owner. With a smile, the young man introduced himself. The pharmacist said nothing, but came out from behind the counter and took the young salesman by the coat collar and literally threw him out of the store, telling him not to come back.

The young salesman had a lot of trouble convincing himself to make a second call that day, but he did.

Wandell Allegood who'd been treated just as rudely as the young man by that druggist delights in telling the "rest of the story." In Wandell's words, "That young man decided he wasn't going to let that ill-tempered druggist run his life. Twenty years later, the young man was one of the most successful business people in our area. That pharmacist? He had to close his store for lack of customers. We haven't heard anything about him in years."

(Hook Spots)

Howard Drobney completed the curriculum at Brown Institute in Minneapolis-St. Paul after service in the Korean War.

He worked for two stations, KWAT (Watertown, South Dakota) and KDLM (Detroit Lakes, Minnesota). His third station was KGDE, Fergus Falls, Minnesota. The station, started in 1926 by pharmacist Charles Jaren, had been sold in 1946 to a prominent Fergus Falls family, the Dells.

One of the family members was a judge on the state supreme court.

When Howard arrived at KGDE, he was assigned an announcing shift and given a stack of ads that had been clipped from the town's daily newspaper. He was instructed during his off-the-air hours to call on those merchants and sell them radio advertising.

He recalls, "The radio station had been in business so long that most businesses had advertised on it. It was not hard selling."

There was no copy written. When you sold a customer, you hung his newspaper ad on a hook in the control room. You adlibbed from it, when the log called for "a hook spot." He remembers, "I didn't have any trouble selling ads or adlibbing them, but, I must admit, I was a little embarrassed talking about women's underwear for the lingerie shop that I sold regularly."

At KGDE, announcers did not get a commission for selling those "hook spots." It was part of the "pretty low paying job."

Howard left KGDE because "there wasn't much present there or much future either working for the Dells." He switched careers, going into law enforcement. He had some experience in that during his years in the service. He spent the rest of his working life at Minnetonka, Minnesota, a "Twin Cities" suburb. The last twelve years of his working life, he was chief of that 40-officer police department.

(Agreeing With the Customers)

Many years ago, I asked a friend of mine about his sales manager. He told me, "I had to let him go. He was agreeing with the customers. I can't have that."

There's an entirely different view of that now. Gary Fuller, long at WZMG, Opelika and WKKR, Auburn, Alabama, says, "When a customer says he doesn't like the music we play on our stations, I tell him, I don't either, but I don't like worms. I take worms with me when I go fishing, because that's what the fish like."

(A Radio Sales Oddity)

Jim Davidson made a good living by researching, writing, voicing, and selling a 5-minute daily program he syndicated called, "The Way to Live Your Life." His best customers were funeral homes.

(Keeping 'Em Sold)

"It's what happens after you sell 'em that's important," Paul "Moon" Mullins says. It's been almost 20 years since he's been on WPFB, between Cincinnati and Dayton, at Middletown, but his listeners still remember him telling them:

"Go to Bud's Market in (suburban) Dayton for your fruits and vegetables. Ten thousand flies can't be wrong."

"Bentley's Radiator Shop in Middletown is the best place to take a leak."

"At Homer's I.G.A. in Sprayborn, Ohio, you can get bread three times for a dollar."

Paul's son, Joe, has made radio a Mullins' family tradition. He owns, operates, and is a star personality on Ohio trimulcast WBZI, Xenia; WKFI, Wilmington; and WEDI, Eaton.

(First Things First)

In 25 years, she missed only two days work. Esther Blodgett is remembered for the service she gave her community as owner-operator of WMCR, Harvard, Illinois. She's also remembered for spouting harsh words and carrying a shotgun, running off an FCC inspector. She wrote the FCC, saying she was too busy running her station and selling advertising to fill out forms and host inspectors.

John Russell Ghrist in "Valley Voices"

INSIDE STUFF

Radio is like no other business. It has to please the government which regulates it, the listeners whose interest it must keep, and advertisers "who pay the bills." We'll take a brief trip behind the scenes. These stories should help you appreciate the folks you probably hear little about, but they make the "magic that is radio happen."

(The Engineer's Secret)

Walker Carver was the Chief Engineer and News Director of WBCU, Union, South Carolina, from the 1950s to the mid-1970s. His fellow staff members always wondered about what he really did.

Often, they called him when a problem arose that took the station off the air. Very often that problem was in the control board in the station's studio control room.

When he was called, Walker showed up with his trademark "bag of tools." To the person on duty, he would always say, "Go out in the lobby while I get this straightened out." Ralph Greer, a fellow staffer and very warm friend of Carver, remembers one day when the incident repeated itself. He went into the lobby as Carver requested, then Greer peaked through the control room window. He saw Carver aiming very carefully, and then kicking a certain spot on the control board. Presto! The control board came back to service.

Carver never told anyone exactly where that spot was.

(A Trusty Hammer)

An "old" Pennsylvania radio hand, Cary Simpson, at one of the stations he has owned and operated for a long time, tells of a "little hammer" on a string tied to the remote control unit in the studio. When some of the unit's controls failed to operate, a gentle tap of the little hammer would magically correct the problem. Cary has claimed for years, he didn't know why the little hammer "did the trick." Those kinds of engineering "secrets" are frustrating to legions of us "non-engineering types."

(The Broom Slipped)

Rick Charles—longtime owner/operator of WRJC AM/FM, Mauston, Wisconsin—remembers, early in his sales career, the door on the back of the Gates Transmitter was rigged for safety so that if it was opened, the transmitter went off. At the station where Rick was working, the transmitter door latch was undependable, so the engineer installed a broom handle with the door on one end, a wall on the other. This kept the transmitter door from opening accidentally and turning the station off.

Rick remembers driving one of his customers back to his store after "a power lunch." As they were riding along, the station went off the air. The customer asked Rick what had happened. His answer, "Somebody must have bumped into the broom handle that keeps the transmitter on the air."

Decades later, the customer still does business with Rick and often asks, "Is somebody at the station watching the broom handle?"

(What's It Worth?)

How much is a radio ad worth? That question is as old as commercial radio broadcasting itself.

In 1957, fabled Georgia broadcaster Mike McDougal was doing very well as sales manager of WRFC in Athens, Georgia, but he wanted a station of his own. He got a construction permit for WCHK at Canton, Georgia. The building came along as scheduled. Mike set a target date to go on the air. He also hired a salesman.

Athens, where Mike was working, was a town of about 100,000. Canton's population is less than 7,000. Mike hired a salesman to pre-sell his new station.

He went to his printer in Athens and made changes in the WRFC rate card. When it came to the prices on the card, Mike told the printer, "Divide them in half. That'll be our rate at WCHK."

The new salesman picked up the rate cards and started calling on customers. A day or so into the effort, Mike found out that someone in the print shop didn't know to cut the prices in half. The new salesman had no idea either. He just went out and sold time. That station had years of very successful history thanks to "those very good rates."

From Rhet Turpenseed's
History of Georgia Radio

(Thank You For Asking Us)

ASCAP, BMI and SESAC hold the rights to all the music played on a radio station. That's been true for years.

It was the policy of ASCAP to write a letter to the licensee of each new radio station granted. A couple of non-broadcasters in Eastern Kentucky obtained a construction permit for a new station. Shortly afterwards, they received the customary ASCAP letter accompanied by a blank contract for them to fill out and sign.

The partners were brand new to the radio business. They knew nothing about music licenses radio stations had to pay. They looked at the letter and sent a response saying, in so many words, "Thank you for your very kind invitation, inviting us to join. We certainly intend to as soon as we can afford it." An

ASCAP field man called on them shortly, pointing out that they couldn't afford not to join. Obviously, they "joined."

(Competition)

One of the Twentieth Century's great merchants was John Cash (J.C.) Penney, who built the department-store chain from one store in Kemmerer, Wyoming, to hundreds all across the country. Penney always said, "The best friend a merchant has is a good competitor."

For forty years, Tommy Patterson operated a station at Martinsville, Virginia. One of his former competitors, years later, still remembers him as a very good broadcaster and a very solid businessman who could have made it in any line of endeavor.

Not only is radio time sold for cash, but also in some instances, a radio station trades its time for goods and services. (That type of arrangement exists in other lines of business as well.)

Tommy Patterson was dead set against selling his radio time for anything except cash. He carried no network programs after they quit paying compensation to affiliates. He would not carry barter-syndicated programming either.

His staff continually hounded him to carry Casey Kasem's "America's Top 40," a barter program. After he had said no on numerous occasions, he decided it was time to bring the discussion to an end.

On payday, instead of a paycheck, each of Mr. Patterson's employees received a crate of apples. All hell broke loose. He calmly explained he was bartering for their services like they wanted him to do for the "Top 40" program. Nobody ever again mentioned bartering for anything.

Phil Weiner
Retired Broadcaster

(Voice Tracking)

Those who manage radio stations must have the same goals as people in any line of business, as one of my non-broadcaster backers told me forty years ago, "You have to cut the cloth to fit the pattern."

One of the newest efficiencies in radio broadcasting is called "Voice Tracking." It is very controversial, but in Vern Kasper's words, "It's not new." Kasper who, for over a half century, has owned stations in Indiana (WILO/WSHW Frankfort) says he did voice tracking as early as 1938. (Vern has had a first ticket since 1936.)

An announcer at a station, where Vern was working as an engineer, believed his wife was "carrying on" with a neighbor while he was at work doing his disc jockey type program. Vern recorded his fellow worker's intros and "outros" so he could "sneak" home to check things out. Yes, his wife was doing what he thought she was doing.

(Very Clean Cars)

When an "Idea Bank" member suddenly left the business, the organization did not have a chairman for its convention in Winston Salem, North Carolina. David Luther was hastily drafted for the honor. He did so well, that by the time he retired as manager of WBTM, Danville, Virginia, he was chosen as Administrator for the "bank."

David remembers that North Carolina convention like it was yesterday—except it's been twenty years. He particularly remembers that town had just gotten its first "topless" car wash. Many of the conventioneers took their cars through it two or three times a day. Most of those cars were rental cars.

(Things Were So Good in New England)

In 1987, the New Hampshire Broadcasters Association canceled an association-sponsored seminar. Only two stations had signed up—the topic: "Stress Management."

(How Lucky Can You Get?)

The Indiana Broadcasters Association has a long tradition of holding a drawing at the final banquet of each convention. Members and associate members donate the prizes for the drawing.

Don Martin, owner/operator of WSLM, Salem, Indiana, about fifty miles from Louisville, Kentucky, had a delinquent advertiser on his books.

It was a West End Louisville funeral home. Don unhappily settled the bill for a gift certificate from that establishment. He donated that gift certificate as a prize for the convention drawing.

Don's prize "stole the show" when it was won by Earl Metzger, manager of WITZ AM/FM, Jasper, Indiana, a licensed funeral director, who left the family funeral business to go into the radio business.

Charlie Jenkins, Former President
Indiana Broadcasters Association
Clear Channel Radio
Louisville, Kentucky

(Glad to Meet You)

A station in the east switched from music to an all-talk format (mainly from satellite.) All of the jocks were fired. When one of them came into the unemployment office, a clerk told him, "I've met all the disc jockeys in town at one time or another. I wondered when I'd get to meet you."

(The Managers)

The folks who run radio stations are as diverse as the stations they manage and the cities and towns where they operate. Here are some quotes, I thought worth including, from a cross-section of them:

(Going Broke Gracefully)

A West Virginia broadcaster had just gone broke "gracefully" when I talked to him. He shared this advice: "Don't worry about your enemies. They really don't know much about you; worry about your friends—they always know too much."

(Always Listen)

Bill Crain was a southern Illinois funeral director (six locations). When he successfully survived cancer, he decided to fulfill a life's dream. He bought WKRO, Cairo, Illinois. He said, "Always listen when someone is talking. You'll either learn something, or find out that he's a damn fool."

(How Bad Is It?)

During the Midwest "farm crises" of the eighties, my career-long friend, the late Paul Olsen, was the longtime owner of KLEM/KZZL, LeMars, Iowa. He said, "Business is so bad, even people who don't ever intend to pay aren't buying."

(It's All—)

Allan Land, WHIZ AM/FM/TV at Zanesville, Ohio, says he has "Three Rules."

Rule #1. Don't sweat the small stuff.

Rule #2. It's all small stuff.

Rule #3. If you can't fight—learn to flee."

(Trials of Management)

During his years managing stations in the Pittsburgh area, Mel Goldberg lamented, "When I'm right, nobody remembers. When I'm wrong, nobody forgets."

(Don't)

"Don't let your competition run your station. Above all, don't let them set your rates."
Houston Pearce
New South Radio
Tuscaloosa, Alabama

(Imagination)

Curt Brown, the longtime, very successful manager of KTTS, Springfield, Missouri, often said:

"I want everybody in our station to use his or her imagination—EXCEPT THE BOOKKEEPER."

GETTING FIRED

I imagine many of you who read the "Inside Stuff" pages may be contemplating a career in radio.

I don't have any priceless advice, or, for that matter, little that is of any real value. However, if you want to make it really big, be ready to get fired.

Bill Hartnett, longtime radio and TV guy, now retired in Cincinnati, tells the story of coming home one evening. "My wife took one look at me and said, 'You've been fired.'"

Before he could answer her, a former colleague and friend called on the phone, telling Bill that a terrible thing had just happened. One of his newscasters had quit without notice. "He said he was desperate to find a replacement," asking if Bill knew of anyone.

Bill answered that he did know of someone—himself. The station was WOWO, Fort Wayne, Indiana. His friend and boss was news director Abe Albright. The job lasted three years.

Sometime during your career, you may have to fire someone yourself. I doubt that you'll like doing it. In 40 years, Walter May has expanded from a single 250-watt station to 8 radio stations in the Pikeville, Kentucky/Williamson, West Virginia area. He claims he's never fired anyone. When an employee comes up short, Walter calls him into his office saying, "I'm sorry you've decided to quit." If he says he hasn't, Walter calmly spells out his shortcomings, adding that no one who wanted to keep a job would do such things.

All the really big-time radio people, it seems, have been fired. Examples:

(Dr. Laura)

At this writing, Dr. Laura Schlessinger has the second largest audience in talk radio (bested only by Rush Limbaugh). Her program, unlike most of the "heavy hitters" in talk radio, is not right- or left-wing political, but focuses on issues of the heart, marital problems, child rearing, questions of morality, and integrity. The Doctor is a real doctor holding a doctorate in psychology, and she has other advanced degrees.

She's been on the air since the '70s, but had not been a big success. In 1995, she was not on the air, and her contract as a faculty member at University of Southern California had not been renewed. In effect, the University fired her.

She was then hired by KFI, Los Angeles, the radio station with the most far reaching daytime signal in the nation. Her advice, often mixed with doses of "tough love," made her an instant local success. She was then picked up coast-to-coast.

She is a lady of strong opinion and often the subject of controversy—but she's never dull.

(Arthur Godfrey)

He was a mega success in the late 1940s and early 1950s. He accounted for 10% of all the money the entire corporation made, some years. He claimed he picked up his unique one-to-one style, listening to the radio in his hospital room day after day, getting over injuries of an auto accident He was, at the time, a not-impressively-paid staff announcer at NBC, Washington. When he went back to work and told his NBC bosses he thought radio with its formality—even pomposity—was "doing things wrong," they fired him. He went to CBS where he was successful beyond belief for several years.

(Larry King)

His four-hour, midday talk show on WIOD, Miami, over time attracted a dizzying array of high profile celebrities: Don Rickles, Ella Fitzgerald, Danny Thomas, Lenny Bruce, Jimmy Hoffa, etc.

After a failed marriage to a Playboy Bunny, King began spending three times what he was making, was arrested for misusing $5,000 belonging to a business associate, and was drowning in debt. He declared bankruptcy. King's station fired him, and he also lost his TV and newspaper part-time, but lucrative, jobs. He was out of radio for four years when Ed Little and the Mutual Network took a chance on him in 1978.

(Don Imus)

The "I Man" was fired by WNBC in New York in 1977. He was said to be unreliable and uncontrollable at the time. He put his life back together and returned in 1979 to WNBC (now WFAN). His show is also carried across the country on a special network. Being a guest on his show is a "must" for political figures of all stripes.

(Wally Phillips)

Although New York and Los Angeles are larger radio markets, Phillips in Chicago, the #3 radio market, topped not only all of his local competition, but L.A. and "Big Apple" morning disc jockeys too. He had an amazing 400,000 listeners a quarter hour in the 1970s. He was the most listened to local radio personality in the nation.

Phillips after World War II service attended Shuster Martin Drama School in his hometown of Cincinnati. Bruce Grant, another Cincinnatian, was a classmate. He helped Wally get a job at Grand Rapids on WJEF. Grant enjoyed a half-century of unequaled morning-show success in West Michigan.

In 1948, Wally Phillips landed back in his hometown. His career seemed unspectacular there for the first couple of years. He was several times unemployed, then in 1950, he was hired by WCPO where he did afternoon "drive" and a two-hour, late evening show from a popular downtown restaurant/bar.

One evening in 1952, he let loose on the evening show with very critical remarks about his station's management. He was fired!

Phillips had a devoted following who let loose a heavy barrage of "Letters to the Editor," begging the Cincinnati radio establishment to put him back on the air.

Ward Quaal was managing WLW and its TV stations at that time. Quaal told the papers, "If so many people want him on the air, we'll put him on WLW."

When Quaal was hired to run WGN Radio and Television in Chicago in 1956, he took Phillips with him.

(Jean Shepherd)

In a three-year span, Jean Shepherd worked for three of Cincinnati's four major radio stations. There and elsewhere, his unique way of doing things got him into trouble with station managements.

Finally, in 1957, he landed on a station in a place where his unpredictable style would find a devoted following. The station was WOR. The place was New York City. He mesmerized thousands of listeners with his unique brand of storytelling. Remarkably, his several hour nightly broadcasts were done without script, or even notes.

Shepherd's popularity extended beyond the New York area and even beyond his lifetime. A decade after his death, his recordings, books, and stage plays enjoy a huge "cult" following. His works include such diverse offerings as "A Christmas Story" and "In God We Trust—All Others Pay Cash."

(Highest Paid Ever)

Rush Limbaugh, by the turn of the century, was earning more money than any radio performer in the country and in history—more than thirty million dollars a year.

Whether he was going to quit or be fired was a matter of discussion during Rush's time at WIXZ near Pittsburgh. In Pittsburgh at KQV, Rush was fired. After a short time out of work, he changed fields, leaving radio to become a public relations man for the Kansas City "Royals." He then returned to radio at KMBZ in Kansas City, where he was fired in 1984. His career blossomed when he made a change to the West Coast and KFBK, Sacramento.

It was just a short four years between getting fired in Kansas City and being hired to go nationwide on a network, which would grow to over 600 stations, including the biggest, most powerful, most prestigious in the country.

(An Even Bigger Comeback Story)

Ronald Reagan was on his first job after college, announcing at WOC, Davenport, Iowa.

Sometime during his first year, David Palmer, son of the owner and founder, Colonel B.J. Palmer, fired Reagan to hire a more experienced man. When the more experienced man showed up, he refused to work "without a contract." The Colonel refused to give anyone working for him a contract, so, Reagan kept the job and went on to Palmer's bigger station, WHO, Des Moines, where he built a region wide fan base, especially for his sports broadcasts. Five years after he came close to losing his job, he was in Hollywood. Fifty years later, he was the leader of the free world.

Reagan's America
Gary Wills (Doubleday)

GETTING HIRED

For those seeking highly successful radio careers, it's important to remember, you have to get hired before you can get fired. Here are a few classic hiring stories.

(Out of the Gutter)

During his long career as owner/operator of KOGA, Ogallala, Nebraska, Ray Lockhardt says, "I was in a constant recruiting mode. I had my best luck hiring people with natural ability from outside the business." He points to one of his very best:

When the "Holiday Inn" was first opened in Ogalallala, there was a young man who, Ray says, "seemed to be a jack of all trades. I got to know him, and realized, though not trained, he had a great radio voice. When I had an opening, I asked him to try for it. As I expected, he was great reading commercials and doing newscasts and sportscasts."

Over the years, he came up through Ray's organization, finally holding the #2 spot, second only to Ray, the station sales manager. When Ray sold out to Clear Channel, they kept John Brandt on, and he's doing, in Ray's words, "a great job."

Every time John got a raise and/or promotion, Ray reminded him of the day he hired him. "When I went to see him, he'd finished his shift at the inn and was at the very back end of the establishment's parking lot. He was washing his car. I always reminded him that I hired him out of the gutter."

(One Man—Two Strange Hiring Stories)

The day he graduated from high school, he wasted no time trying to get a radio job he'd dreamed of during his school years. He drove south from his hometown of Cincinnati to Cynthiana, Kentucky, where his family had roots.

His first stop at WCYN netted the kind of result most young people encounter on their first try.

The station had no openings, but I told him, "Leave me your address and phone number. I'll talk to some of the other small stations in the area. Maybe they have something." I bought him his lunch out of my $10.00 a month expense account. No big deal, the lunch cost $1.25.

After he left, I returned to the station, where the night announcer greeted me. He told me he was quitting and would be starting that afternoon at a local factory. As he left, I picked up the phone and called the number I had just been given. I was embarrassed to tell the young man's mother, "Your son has been here applying for a job. I didn't have an opening a half hour ago, but I have one now. Can you pack him a bag and send him back? I'll put him to work right away."

I gave the office girl (that's what we called them in 1958) a day off for coming in that evening to show my new-hire the "ropes."

He stayed a year and a half and told me he wanted to get into a rated market. I had a friend managing a station outside of Huntington, West Virginia, trying to get his low-power AM into the larger city's ratings. He hired my man who was surprised that that job paid no more than I was paying at our little station in a little town (10 cents above minimum).

He made the most of his spot in a rated market. In less than ten years, he was Program Director of the top station in the country's 50th market, WKLO, Louisville, Kentucky. He was twice chosen as "Program Director of the Year" by the music magazines.

By the mid-'70s, he was program director of a station that

was then a non-entity in the San Antonio market (somewhat bigger than Louisville at the time). He says now, "I was burned out with the schizophrenia of the audience and the "jocks" in "Top 40 Radio." I talked myself into the program directorship of 50,000-watt WOAI, which was moving from music to All Talk." He continues, "John Barger had just been hired to manage what would become the "flagship" of Clear Channel Communications. I had been making $16,000 a year at KONO. Barger made a firm offer of $14,000. When I objected, he said, 'KONO's going nowhere; Talk WOAI is going to be big. You're smart enough to take less money to get in on it.'" He says, "I guess I was because I took it."

In the thirty years since Carl Truman Wigglesworth took that better than 10% salary cut to change from a "rocker and a roller" to a "talker and a seller," he has enjoyed great popularity and a following among San Antonio advertisers that has made him one of the market's top earning radio personalities. In the spring of 2005, he became a partner with John Barger and others, in the market's fifth "talk" station, KAHL.

(Making the Most of It)

He was wounded in the 1943 North African Campaign of World War II. When he returned to his hometown of Cincinnati, he enrolled at the city's College—Conservatory of Music. In 1947, his voice coach told him that WLW was going to hire a host for a new all-night disc jockey program. "That's something you could do," she told him. "You ought to apply for that job." He did!

In the 1930s, WLW had operated with a half-million watts. Its advertising rates were as high as those charged by major New York stations. The station had given birth to so many nationally famous entertainers that it was called the "Cradle of the Stars." People who wanted to be announcers there had to be very, very good and have at least five years' experience.

Bill Nimmo got an interview and audition there. He passed the very demanding audition with "flying colors." During his interview, he was asked a wide range of questions. The matter of experience came up only once. Matter of factly, one of the executives asked him, "You do have experience, don't you?" Nimmo answered, "Yes, I was on Armed Forces Radio." The questioner changed the conversation. Nimmo was hired.

Over the next five years, he would become one of the WLW stars in the "cradle." Afterward, he went to New York where he did all manners of network shows and other performances. He returned to Cincinnati in the 1960s, where he was an instructor at his alma mater. The experience referred to in his WLW interview consisted of an AFRS interview about his battle injuries. It had lasted, he says, "no more than 45 seconds."

(I Can)

Bob Schieffer of CBS Radio and TV got his first broadcast job in the '60s at KXOL, Fort Worth, Texas. He was in college.

The station was across the street from a high school football stadium. Bill Hightower asked him to describe that stadium. Bob remembers, "I did a bad job, but apparently, it was good enough for Bill to give me the $1.25 an hour job."

When asked if he could type, he said, "Yes. I followed Sammy Sneed's golf advice, 'If you don't know how to putt, play for $100 a putt. You'll learn soon enough."

This Just In (Putnam)

WE'VE GOT NEWS FOR YOU

News is an important part of what makes a terrestrial radio station more than a "juke box." It's what keeps folks in tune with their neighborhood and their world. Radio station news operations, from time to time, have made their station people proud and sometimes a little bit embarrassed. We share a few of those embarrassing moments here.

(Too Successful)

The Bartels were proud of their Milwaukee station. It not only served up hit music hosted by the town's best disc jockeys, it was also the city's spot for breaking news. The brewing capital of the world was in tune and turned on to WOKY in the 1960s. WOKY was on top of the city's fires, traffic accidents, and criminal activities.

The high point came during a huge summer parade as WOKY tracked the travel of a suspected killer through the crowded streets. The low point came the same day as a WOKY newsman came on the air with, "Undercover agents for Milwaukee's finest have a suspected drug dealer under surveillance, sitting at the bar at Pete's Tavern, Sixteenth and Wisconsin. As soon as the drug transaction is completed, both parties will be arrested."

As luck (bad luck) would have it, the radio on the bar at Pete's was tuned to WOKY. It was playing loudly. The would-be arrested drug dealer and his prospective customer heard the report, got up, looked at the other two men at the bar, saluted and left.

Terry Metheney, Retired Broadcaster
Van Buren, Arkansas

(We Were Took)

"The WHKP, Hendersonville, North Carolina, staff had been snowbound all day. The program director was out with the flu; two of our regular announcers were unable to get to the station. One of our announcers was at the City Hall covering the local election. The one announcer at the studio was our least experienced man. He was 'covered up' answering phone calls: 'Will the schools be open tomorrow?'—'How deep is the snow?'—'How are the roads?'—'Are you telling people to feed the birds?'

"And then, the big call comes in. 'Someone,' our harried announcer is told, 'has made off with the ballot box at gunpoint.' Our man, with just a month's radio experience, operating in a high pressure, noisy, chaotic scene, must make a fateful decision—should he break the 'big story.' He does.

"Frantically, the local police chief hurried to the station to inform our young announcer that the information he received, then broadcast, was false.

"Our aspiring 'Winchell' was 'sorry' for his mistake in not checking the false story before broadcasting it. His apology was so sincere; we knew he'd live down the embarrassment quickly. He did!"

Art Cooley, President
WHKP
Hendersonville, North Carolina

(Under What?)

A policeman in arresting a motorist told a local radio station that the subject was under the "affluence of alcohol."

(Governor's Conference)

"The parade will follow just as soon as the governors are loaded."

(The Simpsons of Pennsylvania)

Cary Simpson and his late wife, Betty, delighted in telling their early "fluffs" on the air. Samples:

"The funeral service will be held tomorrow. He's been dead for the last six months."

And Cary tells of Betty reporting on the Rainbow Girls on the local news. She identified one of the young ladies as "Miss Immorality," instead of "Miss Immortality."

(Frosty in Iowa)

Now retired, he was known as one of the premier broadcasters in Iowa, although he headquartered in the little town of Grinnell. In his hometown, he was known for his daily local news broadcasts on KGRN. A real pro, he seldom "fluffed." When he did, it was always worth hearing.

In reporting on a rape in Des Moines, he said, "The victim told police the assault took place on Grand Avenue, but they said it actually took place on Locust Street." Frosty recapped the story thusly, "Des Moines woman assaulted on Locust—though it was Grand."

And, when the Safeway Supermarket closed its doors in Grinnell, Frosty recapped that story with, "There's no Safeway in Grinnell."

Frosty's Daughter
Dorea Potter
KWON/KRIG/KYFM
Bartlesville, Oklahoma

(Promoting Culture)

A west coast station closed an evening newscast with, "We remind you to enjoy the Arts Series tonight. Tonight's feature will be the classic film, *Of Human Bandage.*

(A Few Weather Reports Worth Noting)

"Thunder showers Friday, probably followed by Saturday."

On KHAR, Anchorage, Alaska: "Helena got six inches last night. That's Helena, Montana—and that's snow."

Another forecast called for "Rowdy followed by clain." (*Cloudy* followed by *rain.*)

(A Stroke of the Old Master)

Jim Carroll, who owns a group of radio stations in the West, was a McLendon newscaster in the 1960s. He remembers this classic McLendon story:

On a typical KLIF (Dallas) fast-paced, over-storied newscast, Carroll signaled for the engineer to play the next tape. Instead of the voice of a newsmaker, a burst of profanity came over the air. McLendon heard it. He rushed into the recording studio where he made a dramatic, recorded apology. The emotional message told listeners how sorry the station was for the error that had happened. He did not say for what he was apologizing. That apology ran every hour for 24 hours. Although few people noticed the mistake, everybody noticed the apology. It was the topic of conversation in the Dallas-Fort Worth area for days.

RADIO PERSONALITIES

(Sometimes Not Real)

Back in the 1970s, listeners in the Waco-Temple area heard Paul Harvey, News at 7:30, then "Miss Lillian's Help Line" at twenty-five minutes to eight.

"Miss Lillian" answered her mail—some real, some not—asking for advice or information. Here are a couple of typical broadcasts:

LISTENER: "Dear Miss Lillian, I understand it's against the law in Russia to name a baby girl 'Ruth.' Is that true?"

MISS LILLIAN: "Yes, because Russians are ruthless."

And another:

LISTENER: "Dear Miss Lillian, I understand there was a 'lady of the evening' who operated years ago in Waco and Temple. She eluded authorities for years. In more recent years, she's written a book about her experiences. Please name the book."

MISS LILLIAN: *A Tail of Two Cities*

And this one, which Paul Harvey told on his programs:

LISTENER: "I hear that Toyota and Chevrolet are going into a joint venture to build a car together. What are they going to call it?"

MISS LILLIAN: "They're going to use three letters of each name—it'll be a TOY-LET."

Miss Lillian was not real. The voice was made up by morning-man Steve Cannon. It was written, (sometimes the letters too) as well as the answers, from Miss Lillian by Lynn Woolley. She hasn't been on the Waco station for years, but there are still a lot of seventies-era radio listeners who think she was real—and miss her.

Last Great Days of Radio
Lynn Woolley
Republic of Texas Press

(She Was Real)

In 1989, the National Association of Broadcasters held its first annual gala, "The Marconi Awards." Radio's brightest stars were paraded before a giant hall filled to capacity by the industry leaders. The show was stolen that night by "a little old lady" from an Iowa town of 5,000. Billie Oakley was 72 then, the hostess of "Kitchen Klatter," sponsored by a Shenandoah firm that made flour flavorings. The program was not only heard on KMA, but it was also heard on 22 other stations in the Midwest.

Billie delighted the audience of radio's top executives when she told them that although she'd been in radio for almost forty years, the 1969 convention was the first radio convention she'd ever attended. She got a tremendous laugh when she said, "I remember when the managers of our station used to come back to the station all tired out. This convention-going is hard work; isn't it?"

Billie Oakley started to work at 14 at KMA. She worked her way up to the "Kitchen Klatter" hostess spot. After the big national award, she stayed with the program for three more years. When "Kitchen Klatter's" sponsor opted to try a new advertising tact, Billie decided to try something different herself. She left radio at 75 years young and lived in retirement into her nineties. She's still remembered by faithful listeners so long ago, and Kermit Schafer immortalized her in his book, *Prize Bloopers* (Avenel):

On "Kitchen Klatter," Billie told her far-flung audience how much she liked to receive mail. "I like going to bed at night with a handful of mail." After some titters from the studio crew, she quickly explained, "Okay fellas, that's M-A-I-L."

(Also Very Real)

Her son, Ed, owned and managed the radio station when she arrived in Union, South Carolina. Exactly how it happened, no one seems to remember, but Elize hosted a one-hour program every morning on WBCU. She'd never done anything like that, but co-workers and town's people give her high marks for her natural, pleasant voice with just a tinge of a New Orleans accent. She came across as warm and understanding—not preachy.

She gave recipes, household hints, fashion tips. She had very good taste in music. One of the features every morning was the playing of a Hawaiian song. It was a favorite of her housewife audience. Few had ever been there, and very few had any prospect of visiting there. It was a dream—a pleasant one.

Like "Miss Lillian" in Texas and Billie in Iowa, Elize took some things seriously—but not herself. A co-worker remembers Elize reading a story on her program about Civil War hero David Farragut. He is best remembered, the article said, for saying, "Damn the torpedoes and full speed ahead."

After reading that, with her microphone still on, she asked Ralph Greer who was running the controls, "Ralph, can you say *damn* on the air?" He hadn't heard the question. She repeated, "Ralph, can you say *damn* on the air?" This time he heard her and merely shrugged. She ended the whole matter saying, "Well, the admiral did say it."

WE NOW LEAVE OUR STUDIOS

Remote broadcasts are not for the faint of heart. Such broadcasts are prone to accidents—often embarrassing.

One of the classic remote broadcast "disasters" took place back in the "golden age of radio." It happened under the auspices of the most prestigious firm in the radio industry—NBC.

The senior radio network sent a broadcast crew to Capistrano to broadcast the swallows leaving there. All the equipment was set up. The nation waited with bated breath to hear the sound of millions of whirring wings. Nothing happened.

The swallows had left a day early.

H. Allen Smith as quoted in
The Great American Broadcast
Leonard Maltin (Dutton)

Here are some stories about remotes: good, bad, and ugly. We'll let you grade them.

(Spectacular)

WTBF, Troy, Alabama, has a 17-foot helium blimp. After years in service, it still draws a big crowd whenever it is sent up.

On one occasion, the blimp got away from its 250-foot rope. It went up 500 feet, 1,000 feet, 1,500 feet, 2,000 feet. It was out of sight.

Jim Rolling, co-owner and manager of WTBF, says, "'Up Up and Away' was one of my favorite songs back in the '60s. But, it's not an enjoyable song when it's your blimp.

"An all-points bulletin was sent out by area law enforcement agencies. Twenty-four hours later, it was seen 15 miles north of town. It disappeared. Then, two weeks later I spotted it. It had finally come down on a farm. We got a lot of good, free publicity during the two weeks the blimp was lost," Jim says. "Local folks had a lot of happy memories invested in the blimp. Finding it was like finding an old friend."

(All Wet)

Another WTBF remote "gone bad" didn't end up as happily as the "blimp" story. The station had set up in the gazebo at the local "Bi-Centennial Park." The crowd had assembled. The Memorial Day program was about to begin. The WTBF combination broadcast/public address equipment was turned on.

The transmitter button, through an engineering fluke, started the park sprinkler system. As the "Memorial Day" program started, the crowd was drenched.

(What a Surprise)

Mark Allen, now president of the Washington State Broadcasters Association, was an on-air personality on his first job in Spokane. He'd been sent out to one of the city's malls to do a "Back to School" remote. He was giving it his all on four cut-ins per hour from noon to 6 PM.

When Mark came on with his 4:50 cut-in, he noticed that a lot of people were leaving. At 5:10, he says, "I was going on and on about the great back-to-school specials being offered. A sales clerk from one of the stores came by my microphone. I decided to stop her. Big mistake! She informed me, and all the listeners, that the mall had closed at 5:00."

(Damn Liar)

Phil LeMense, longtime radio guy in the Kalamazoo market, remembers doing a remote on a very rainy afternoon. The host on the remote is supposed to talk up the event and bring a crowd in.

A man and his family come close to Phil's microphone. He's soaked to the skin. His wife's hairdo has been ruined. The kids are bawling. Phil tells the radio audience and the family within earshot, "There's a patch of clear sky in the west. Come on out."

The man of the family gives Phil a nasty stare, and says loudly, "You're a damn liar." Phil was not quick enough at the switch. It went on the air!

(Challenges)

Laurie Prax, manager/co-owner of KVAK, Valdez, Alaska, broadcast live from the "Earthquake Cottage" during a simulated 5.0 earthquake. Afterward, she said, "It was too real-like."

She broadcast live from the back of a snowmobile during a Snow Cross Race Event.

To top that, she provided play-by-play on May Day from the backseat of an aerobatic airplane. Randy Maag, the event organizer, told her before she went up in the plane, "We think it would be cool if you got sick on the air." She says, "I didn't."

(A Movie on the Radio)

It's another heartwarming idea from Valdez, Alaska. Three hundred thirty (330) inches of snow fall there every winter. For ten years, there's been a winter carnival. It's called "Frosty Fever." Auto and truck drivers can view a movie projected on a snow bank. Listeners watch the movie from their vehicles in the community parking lot. KVAK broadcasts the movie sound on the station. Admission is $5.00 per carload. Let it snow! Let it snow!

(Love Finds a Way)

At WIXE, twenty-five miles from Charlotte in Monroe, North Carolina, "Old Radio Guy" Bob Rogers serves up country classics at noontime. When he started courting the station's telemarketer, Betty Love, the community "fell in love with love." When Bob and Betty married, the station broadcast the nuptials live.

Eight hundred dollars worth of congratulatory messages were purchased by local businesses.

(Advertisers with a Personal Interest)

When a new $5-million jail held its open house at Centre, Texas, it was a real boon to the local economy. It also might have been one of the great radio sales stories of all time. Jack Bell, KDET, sold the "Open House" to three local law firms.

(Accident Prone?)

Running a small-town radio station during World War II was, to say the least, very tough. There was a severe shortage of qualified (even not qualified) radio announcers. What is now KHUB, Fremont, Nebraska, had gone on the air in 1939. It struggled through World War II. When the war ended, the station operators, when an opening occurred, found themselves in a very unusual position. They had several qualified candidates. They chose the one they thought was a "real find."

To show off their "find," they sold two remotes the first week to be conducted by the newcomer.

Back in those days, remote gear was in a backpack. It was heavy and uncomfortable. On the first remote, the station's new star accidentally stood in a puddle of water. When he switched on his gear, the first thing the audience heard was "Damn that hurts."

On the second remote, "new star" came down a flight of steps. To steady himself, he reached for the iron railing. He got a shock again, this time yelling, "Ah shit!"

Hal Widsen
KWED, Seguin, Texas
(He started his career at the Fremont station where this story is part of station lore.)

(The Sky's the Limit)

The chain convenience store had been a very hard sell for WPKO/WBLL, Bellefontaine, Ohio. When they finally said yes, Lou Vito, then a new owner/operator, decided it would be a promotion the advertiser would never forget.

Lou bought a quantity of Nerf balls. He hired a pilot and small plane to drop the balls onto the convenience store parking lot. The balls were numbered. People, who picked them up, took them into the store where they'd be redeemed for prizes like free gasoline, snack items, and the grand prize, a power lawn mower.

When the pilot started dropping the balls, many of them got caught up in the plane's propeller. The grand-prize winning ball showed up a half mile from its intended target. A man mowing his lawn with his own power mower was the grand prizewinner. He had no idea what was going on, but he took the prize mower.

When people listening to the event on the radio heard what was happening, they hurriedly drove to the convenience store. In the town of 12,000, unhappy police officers estimated there was a crowd of 2,000. Additional police had to be brought in to keep order.

Vito was unsuccessful in getting the pilot to call it quits. He made another pass over the store—no more than 100 feet off the ground. Finally, he ran out of Nerf balls and brought the plane down.

Vito called the promotion "too successful." It was unnerving, but it was indeed "unforgettable."

(Catching 'em Off Guard)

As he read the "gripe" column in *Yank* magazine, he was amazed how funny the average person could be, if he or she was anonymous. On radio, he observed, people became rigid and tense before a microphone. His idea: Secretly record interviews then advise the person that he or she had been recorded for broadcast.

John Dunning in *Encyclopedia of Old Time Radio* (Oxford) says almost everyone was a good sport about it and cooperated, being promised anonymity, $15.00, and the thrill of being on the radio.

The first two interviews took place in a rented office. The first subject was a man who'd been called to paint a sign. His name was Lester Cannon. That's the name he was to paint on the office door window. After considerable haggling, he agreed to do it if the spelling was changed to Lester Kannon.

The second subject was a locksmith, called to free a secretary, who'd been chained to her desk. He was told she never got anything done unless she was shackled. The locksmith freed her, collected his fee and advised Allen Funt, *Candid Microphone* and *Candid Camera* creator, "You better not get caught doing this."

RADIO HOAXES

Orson Wells' 1938 "Mercury Theatre" broadcast vividly demonstrated radio's ability to capture the imagination of its audience.

Wells and the other participants were as astounded as everyone else at the chaos that the radio drama set off across the country. That event set up what radio people would thereafter call, "The Theatre of the Mind."

That chapter in the dramatic series has never been equaled in impact. Wells and his supporters at the time claimed that the adaptation of the H.G. Wells classic *War of the Worlds* was no more than skillful performance of a powerful drama. They meant no harm. The program was in keeping with Halloween.

We have collected some radio "hoaxes." All have had some impact in their areas—none of the proportion of the 1938 program. But, they demonstrate what a powerful impression something special on the radio can make.

(That Town That Was Slandered)

The irreverent *Village Voice* out of the Greenwich Village section of New York City ran a story describing the residents of Tyrone, Pennsylvania, as "rat faced and pea brained."

Among the citizens of the town of 5,500 were Cary and Betty Simpson who owned and operated a group of small radio stations, including the local station WTRN. They were angered by the story that came out of the big city. The Simpsons and WTRN took the lead in settling the score by staging an imaginary "Rat Parade."

In the imaginary parade, there was a "Rats Are Us" float. There was a "Mus-crat" marching band. A "Ratman and Robin" mobile appeared. A downtown merchant who was elected "King Rat" served as parade marshal of the make-believe parade broadcast on WTRN.

The fictitious parade got nationwide publicity and Tyrone got even.

(May I Have This Dance?)

At the end of the "big band era," in the late 1950s, Charlie Stratton, manager of WKOA, Hopkinsville in Western Kentucky, decided to give his listeners a demonstration of radio as the "Theatre of the Mind."

Using sound effects like people engaged in small talk chatter, clinking glasses, even some plates being broken, WKOA created the "Colonial Ballroom."

Each day at noon, lunchtime, radio listeners heard two name bands performing from a revolving bandstand. The first half hour might be Les Brown and his Band of Renown. As they faded away, the make-believe bandstand brought a band like Xavier Cugat upfront with his South American melodies.

The town of 25,000 was unlikely ever to attract one such band, let alone two. Yet, the station started receiving phone calls asking for directions to the "Colonial Ballroom."

(Spotted)

Longtime Kentucky radio personality Russ Hatter was starting his long radio career in the 1960s in Eastern Kentucky at WGOH, Grayson. On his early show, he announced that an "oryx" had been spotted in Carter County.

Area law enforcement officers went into the dictionary to find out what callers were talking about when they reported seeing it. There was no such thing in the dictionary.

Hatter informed a young lawman that there was no "oryx" loose in the county. In fact, there was no such thing as an "oryx." In the words of radio's Senator Claghorn on the 1940s Fred Allen Show, it was "just a hoax, son."

(A Personal Story)

In central Kentucky, I had just taken over as manager of WFKY in Frankfort. I was fortunate to inherit from the previous management a talented young fellow named Fred Gooding. I made him operations manager. I asked him to bring me some ideas.

Over lunch, he told me about a project he'd completed while attending the Radio-TV Arts Department at the University of Kentucky. His project was a reenactment of the "War of the Worlds" 1938 broadcast. He had changed the places to places in the Frankfort area.

He offered to let me broadcast it. I decided it would spark some talk in the community, and we'd find out how many people were listening at night. Television was still new enough that a lot of potential advertisers thought everybody was watching TV at night because they were.

I had been running a daytime station for four years and was out of touch with selling nighttime.

I thought this was a good experiment.

The broadcast was scheduled for ten o'clock on Saturday night. There were no promotional announcements or mentions of any kind before the broadcast was to be run. There were announcements, as there had been in 1938 at the beginning and middle of the program, saying that it was fiction.

I had lived in Frankfort for less than two months—too soon

to be in the telephone book. Yet, while the broadcast was on the air, a half dozen people had taken the time to call information for my new number to call me about the program. Twice that many calls were made to the studio downtown.

Even though everyone (I thought) had heard about the 1938 "War of the World's" broadcast, 26 years before, there were people who thought what was going on, on the radio, was real.

There were some people who thought the broadcast was in bad taste. A few thought it was a funny stunt.

After the reaction we got, I was satisfied that advertising after six o'clock was a good value.

Fred Gooding left within the year, pursuing good jobs in Cincinnati, Little Rock, and Portland, Oregon. He returned to his hometown in middle age to become an executive in state government.

(Telephone Hoax)

Disc jockeys are known to become bored. The central character in this story decided he could beat boredom by staging an outrageous "hoax" on his afternoon show. Bob Spradlin, who was managing WMST, Mount Sterling, Kentucky, at the time, tells us that the caper was carried off without his or anyone else in authority's permission.

The disc jockey announced, "The telephone company has advised us that they are going to clean out their lines. Everyone is advised to place the cradle of their phone in a trash can, so that dust and dirt from the lines would be contained when forced out of the lines."

So many people followed the deejay's prank instructions that the local phone system became overloaded. For a short time, the community was without phone service.

"A couple of phone company executives came in to see me. They came in to properly chastise me for not having better control of my employees. They also wanted assurances that the 'stunt' would not happen again," Spradlin remembers. He continues, "I had a sense that the telephone men were having a hard time containing themselves. It was pretty funny, really."

(Not on Purpose)

In 1933, WIND was in Gary, Indiana, south of Chicago. It accidentally perpetrated one of the all-time great radio hoaxes.

John Dillinger, bank robber and accused "cop killer," was reportedly someplace in the area. A search was undertaken in a forest near Chesterton. On the scene was an impatient Steve Trumball of WIND. He persuaded a policeman to turn on his siren and cause his motorcycle to backfire.

With the sounds behind him, Trumball told WIND listeners to "Listen to the patter of deadly lead." Officials, hearing the broadcast, sent fifty policemen to the scene. It was a hoax! Trumball was thrown in jail for obstructing justice. When he was released, WIND fired him.

Dillinger was gunned down in Chicago the following year. There was no "on the scene" radio coverage.

John Russell Ghrist
Valley Voices (Crosswords)

LOSING IT

Rick Sellers, owner/manager of KMRY, Cedar Rapids, Iowa, has been collecting radio memorabilia for years. One of his proudest possessions is part of a Lowell Thomas broadcast. He was radio's first evening network newscaster, starting in 1930. He did the program until 1977, when he was 84 years old. All those years, he was required listening for everyone who was serious about speech. He was the best. He had no equal in broadcasting the news; yet, he was human, and once in a while "lost it." Rick supplied this item:

Thomas was reporting on a new book called *Diet or Die* by Mrs. Celeste Guyer, better known to millions of carnival fans as "Dolly Dimples." Thomas told his CBS Radio audience, "She was billed as the most beautiful fat lady. Mrs. Guyer weighed 500 and 50 pounds. Count 'em. 500 and 50 pounds. Now a svelte 122 pounds. She tells how she did it. Following advice of a doctor after a near fart…uh…fatal uh heart attack to diet or die. The secret of effective (giggles became longer)…that her willpower was strengthened by (giggles turn into downright laughter)….Well uh anyhow…she says, 'My fat friends from carnival life died at an early age…later buried from the back of a truck.'"

Those were her own words. Why a truck? 'Because,' said Mrs. Guyer, 'they were too big for a hearse.'(Laughs now are absolutely out of control)…(20 seconds of laughter). Finally, Thomas gets out an "ohhhhhhhh." Mercifully, the announcer comes to his rescue saying: "And, so long until Monday, Lowell. This is Warren Moran reminding you to listen each evening Monday through Friday at this same time for the distinctive news reports of Lowell Thomas. Listen Monday evening for Lowell Thomas and the news."

(A Personal Story)

During my first few months as the most over paid, $50.00 a week, radio announcer anywhere, I was breaking in at my first station, WDLB, Marshfield, Wisconsin. J.P. Adler had booked a crystal-ball reader into one of his three local theatres, the "Relda" (Adler spelled backwards).

A local jeweler had seen the man in action on the Relda stage and offered to sponsor him on the radio while he was in town. On Saturday morning, I was asked to stay over for an hour to do that program.

I got the letters, which he had received, that I was to read to him on the air along with commercials for the jeweler. I took them out into the reception room to look them over.

A few minutes before I was to go on the air, I crossed through the master control room. The chief engineer, Jerry Boos, was on duty. Matter of factly, he told me, "Bob, this Ramar is a fake. He says he knows everything, but he doesn't. "

"Why do you say that?" I asked.

"He just asked me, 'Where's the pencil sharpener?'"

When I looked into the small studio, the baldheaded man was sitting at the table peering into a one foot in diameter "crystal ball." "I lost it!"

It was the longest fifteen minutes of my life, not allowing a laugh to come out, but with a discernable snicker in my voice, I got through the letters and the commercials. I was sure that nobody was happy with my performance. I dreaded a phone call from one of the bosses or the sponsor— somebody. Nobody called.

Later, I found out that the Catholics in the area, whose church's beliefs don't hold kindly with crystal-ball readers, were unhappy with everybody concerned with Ramar's visit to town. Everybody connected wanted to forget the whole thing, even my less-than-adequate appearance on the program.

(Going So Well)

When Hal Widsen joined KOIL in Omaha, Nebraska, he says, "Everything was looking great for Don Burden, then later he would lose his FCC radio licenses in some of the best markets in the United States."

Hal had been hired as Production Manager. "A plumb job for a young guy on the way up," he says.

It was a great start for Hal. The station had hired one of the market's great personalities, Bob Wilson. And, a brand new big advertiser had been signed, Guy's Snack Foods.

The first Guy's ad on the station was on Wilson's program. It was a "live read." Bob hit the copy cold. It started, "Guy's nuts are tender and delicious." Wilson lost it!

Guy's didn't cancel. They and Bob stayed on the air for decades.

(Test! Can You Read This Without "Losing It"?)

When the late Ann Landers, the personal advice icon, was on network radio, the announcer read the letters from listeners seeking advice. It had to be one of radio's toughest assignments. Read it aloud:

"My husband is trying to make me insane. He takes things out of my drawers and hides them on me. I search the house for days. He then puts them back in their place and tells me they were there all along. How can I tell him to leave my drawers alone?"

Signed "D.P."

THE RADIO SHOW MUST GO ON

Most of the time it all sounds so effortless when you're listening, but for the person bringing you the program, it can be quite harrowing.

(A Lot to Do)

Tom Webb was working at WMST, Mount Sterling, Kentucky, as chief engineer-announcer while he was getting his electrical engineering degree at University of Kentucky, 35 miles away in Lexington.

Fifty years later, he remembers, "I used to get to the station at 5:30 for the 6:00 sign-on. There was a lot to do. Sometimes, there was a piece of equipment that needed a repair.

"One morning, the Associated Press machine had nothing on it but uppercase Qs—one after the other. I needed news for the six o'clock program, so I ran the half block to a restaurant, picking up a copy of the *Louisville Courier Journal*. I hurried through it marking the highlights of the most important stories. My wife, listening at home, said she could hear me turning the pages."

(Crappy Weather)

Another task during the 5:30 pre sign-on was recording the weather forecast over the phone from Blue Grass Airport in Lexington. "One morning when I didn't have time to check it before putting it on the air, I introduced the weatherman, then started the tape. I heard, 'Good morning folks, here's your forecast for today.' THEN I HEARD SOMETHING DROP FOLLOWED BY: 'Oh crap, I dropped the script.' THEN THERE WAS A BRIEF PAUSE FOLLOWED BY: 'Let's start over.'"

(Drowning in Trouble)

When Dick and Pat Billings bought KWRT in Booneville, Missouri, in 1986, the first thing they were greeted with was a huge flood covering thousands of acres of the coverage area. Dick quickly decided to cover the disaster by airplane. He sold the reports for $1,200—a lot of money in a small town in 1986—particularly since the flood closed many businesses.

First problem Dick found was that there was no way he could deliver his broadcasts from a plane. Such equipment was not available in the Boonville area. He decided that he'd take a cassette recorder up in the plane, record what he saw, and then bring it back down to the radio station. Problem was that the local airport was closed because of the flood. The closest open airport was 45 miles away. If he flew in and out of Versailles airport, his reports would be over an hour old when they got on the air.

Pat Billings came up with the solution. She made some little parachutes that would be fastened to the cassettes. When the broadcasts were done, they'd be dropped into an open field next to the radio station, and then taken inside for broadcast.

The Billings' two young children served as runners, getting the tapes, and then running them to the station. All of them made it, but one. That one got carried away by a gust of wind into a nearby lake.

It has never been found.

(Operating an Unlicensed Vehicle)

Covering golf tournaments was not a usual thing at WFKY, Frankfort. But, there was a lot of interest in the summer's big tournament, and there was room in the baseball schedule to do it.

To give listeners a close up to the action reports, the station made arrangements to borrow a golf cart from the pro at the country club—seven miles east of the municipal course where the golf event was scheduled. Between the two places, police stopped the unlicensed vehicle and issued a summons to appear in police court.

The judge, snickering, fined Russ Hatter, operator of the vehicle, $20.00 and said, "I enjoyed listening to the tournament."

The station manager paid the fine, thinking the $20.00 was well spent. There was a story plus a picture on the front page of the daily newspaper.

(News on the Side)

In 1958, WVLK went all out to sell itself as a news leader in the Lexington area. The management of the daily newspaper, like most print journalists, had a degree of scorn for the radio station's news effort. When the station's mobile unit overturned during an ice storm, the newspaper carried a picture of the vehicle with the caption, "News on the Side."

(Breaking and Entering)

At WMST, Mount Sterling, Kentucky, Tom Webb remembers, "The priest at the Catholic Church recorded his Monday morning devotion, then brought the tape into the station before broadcast time.

"On one weekend, the priest was out of town. He called Tony Warren, the part-time announcer, long distance telling him to crawl through a partially opened window at the church rectory, where he'd find the tape on the pastor's desk.

"In following the priest's instructions, Tony unwittingly set off a burglar alarm. The police station was two blocks away.

Two policemen arrested Tony for breaking and entering.

"When they reached the priest by long distance, he backed up Tony's story. He was released, and the program got on the air as scheduled on Monday morning."

(You Do What You Have to Do)

During more than a half century in the radio business, he has been Chief Operating Officer of two radio chains, and has been a Vice President of RAB. He successfully "turned around" several troubled radio stations. One duty has not appeared on his resume.

In the early 1950s, Ray Holbrook was program director of WVLK, Lexington, Kentucky. He had, for several years, hired an aspiring local actor to play Santa Claus on the station at Christmastime. Harry Dean Stanton arrived at Ray's office mid-morning, telling him he would not be able to continue his duties as "Santa." He was leaving by auto for the west coast to take a minor part in a movie. Stanton never returned to Lexington. He established himself in Hollywood as a versatile, reliable, character actor.

Did the WVLK "Santa" leaving disappoint the youngsters who eagerly tuned in each day? He did not. Stepping into the void was Ray Holbrook. He did so well that he not only continued to be "Santa" on the radio during his years at WVLK, but also later appeared on WHIR, Danville, Kentucky, and still later on a station in Mississippi. He says, "I never got an extra dime for doing it, but it's one of my happiest radio memories."

(Preview of Things to Come)

It was his first radio job. He was a junior college freshman, working Sunday afternoons on KCLY, Clay Center, Kansas. The town's new radio station was in the same block as one of the town's biggest retail businesses, the local "True Value Hardware" store.

Without warning, fire broke out and immediately went out of control at the hardware store. KCLY, located in the same block, lost electric power. Joe knew that the people in the area would be tuning into the local station to find out what was happening. It was one of the biggest events in years in Clay Center.

On his own initiative, young Joe connected up the battery-powered "mixer" used on ball games by connecting to the telephone line, which connected the studios with the station transmitter. He got a portable record player out of his car. Between news bulletins about the fire, he played an LP from his personal collection, "Chicago's Greatest Hits."

KCLY was a "middle of the road" station, but Joe remembers, "nobody complained." Joe, ten years later, would become major shareholder/operator of KNCK and 100,000-watt KCKS, Concordia, Kansas.

(A Mystery)

It's six-thirty AM. Paul Tinkle is reading the news on WCMT, Martin, Tennessee. Chris Brinkley, the morning disc jockey, has left the control room. When it's time for a break, Brinkley is not in sight, so Tinkle continues to read news. Tinkle hears a loud noise coming from the women's rest room. A faulty doorknob refuses to open.

With his microphone on, Tinkle gets up from the news desk and opens the door. After about a minute of dead air, Brinkley and Tinkle get back to their air work.

There is no explanation to the radio audience. Things like that are better not discussed on a "family station." Nobody's asking the obvious question, "What was Chris Brinkley doing in the women's room? The men's room is right next to it."

(The Biggest Show Must Go On)

In Indiana, few things are more important than high school basketball—it's the biggest show in town. Radio pioneer Don Burton made the point graphically when he recounted the efforts his Muncie station (WLBC) made to get a game on the air. He told the story to Indiana Broadcasters Association history writers.

Burton was set to broadcast an away game with one of Muncie's chief rivals, Marion. He found out that the Marion School Board had outlawed the broadcast of its high school games.

He was not going to disappoint his Muncie fans. He hired two legal stenographers and a man to spot, posting the threesome in the stands. At halftime, they went to the telegraph office and wired an account to WLBC where Burton had installed a telegraph receiver. Burton, using the wired report accompanied by sound effects, described the game on the air. The same procedure was followed for the second half.

When Burton finished his delayed broadcast, he went to a nearby restaurant where he knew the Muncie team was coming for an after-game snack. The restaurant counterman had been listening to the radio broadcast. When the team arrived, he wondered how they'd made the 40-mile trip so fast. Burton never told him.

(Very Tough Times! Very Small Place!)

KGCX had moved from Vida, Montana (population 27), to Wolfe Pointe (population 3,000) in 1929. Things were good until the Depression settled in. C. Howard McDonald in *History of Montana Broadcasting* says Ed Krebsbach kept his station going by holding dances, potluck suppers, and asking for listener donations. It became profitable in 1941 when it moved to Sydney.

RADIO'S DISC JOCKEYS

For the first twenty years of radio's existence, the term "disc jockey" was not in use. In 1940, it appeared for the first time in print when Walter Winchell used it in his column. Radio historians believe that record company executive Jack Kupp coined the phrase. He used it, it is said, because at first the announcers who hosted programs of records had the duty also of controlling the record's sound volume as it went on the air ("riding gain").

(Who Made Believe First)

On February 3, 1935, Martin Block was the standby announcer during the murder trial of Bruno Hauptman, standing accused in the Lindberg baby murder-kidnapping. The trial was being carried live by New York City's, then newest radio station, WNEW. It had come on the air in February the year before.

As the trial proceeded, there were long periods of inactivity. Something had to be done to fill that time. Legend has it that Block, on his own initiative, went to a nearby record store, Liberty Records, and bought records to cover the voids. WNEW had no records in its inventory at the time.

Block played records in quarter-hour segments by one band or one singer. He called it, the "Make Believe Ballroom." When the Hauptman trial was over, WNEW owners decided to keep Block and the "ballroom" on the air.

For Block, the accidental starting of the "Make Believe Ballroom" gave him a permanent place in radio history, made him a millionaire (back when there weren't nearly as many as now), and made him one of radio's top personalities for the next quarter of a century.

But, was Martin Block the creator of the "Make Believe Ballroom" and the radio disc jockey format? "No," say radio history buffs. They point to the fact that Block had first been a commercial announcer on a Mexican border station at Tijuana. That station beamed into San Diego and Los Angeles. Block, after a period of time, went east to New York City, then the nation's center of the radio industry.

While Block was in California, he no doubt heard Al Jarvis on the air at Warner Brothers' station KFWB. Jarvis, as early as 1934, was hosting a program of records for six hours a day. He filled between the records not only with the names of the artists and the titles of the songs, but also tidbits of information about them that he gleaned from trade periodicals. Jarvis called his program, "The world's largest make believe ballroom."

Although Los Angeles is now the nation's largest radio market with the most daily audience and highest advertising revenues, it was not in the 1930s. Ben Torres, author of *The Hits Keep Coming* (Miller-Freeman Books) theorizes that Block got the edge because he was in New York where he got the greatest share of press attention.

But Jarvis did very well. He was on Los Angeles radio and TV into the 1960s.

(Just in Time)

Until the mid-1940s, most radio stations were affiliated with one of the four radio networks. The Mutual Network, the least strong financially, left its member stations with large blocks of unsold time. They often filled them with the disc jockey format. When the post-war period brought hundreds of new stations on the air, many times there was not a network available to them. They put the disc jockey format on their air. Then, when television arrived in the late-1940s, the disc jockey format was an ideal replacement for the big variety shows and dramas that were exiting radio for more lucrative television.

(Disc Jockey—An Endangered Species)

At latest count, there are 76,000 people in the United States working as disc jockey/announcers—about 5 per station. Disc jockeys appearing on more than one station, thanks to the satellite and "voice tracking," have brought about attrition in the profession during the past two decades.

Except in a few stations in large markets, disc jockeys do not have the clout they had in the past glory days. But, it's important to remember how important they still are in terrestrial radio. All of the non-music radio formats on the air garner just a little over 1/5 of radio's daily audience. Music is listeners' number one choice of radio programming—far and away. According to the *Radio Book Directory*, there are 26 music formats on the radio. Only 4 are non-music formats.

In 1941, when Indianapolis' fourth radio station came on the air, its call letters were WISH.

Etched into its tile reception room flooring was the station's slogan, "Anything You Wish." That slogan has certainly come true for radio listeners. In Indianapolis, there are now 40 stations available to the local audience. And that variety is not only in evidence in big cities, but it is also clearly present in the very smallest, most remote places.

(Ant Hill Music)

Howard Hedges is a disc jockey at Homer, Alaska. For ten years, he has hosted a jazz program with the intriguing name, "Jazz to No Where" on KBBI.

One of Hedges most devoted listeners was an elderly gentleman who had lived there since the '50s. He had dubbed Homer, "The Cosmic Hamlet by the Sea."

"He loved Ella Fitzgerald, Sarah Vaughn, Louis Armstrong—particularly songs about the moon," Hedges says.

"During one show, I was in a 'bebop' mood and played several minutes of music by Dizzy Gillespie, Charlie Parker, Miles Davis and the like," he continues.

"The studio phone rang. It was 'Brother Asiah, the Conscience of Our Community' and one of our most devoted fans.

"After exchanging a few pleasantries at the beginning of our phone conversation, he got to the point, asking in his soft gentlemanly voice, 'Brutha, could you lay off that Ant Hill Music?'

"Even though I'd been a musician for years, I had never heard of 'be bop' being referred to in that way. After we finished our conversation, I completely lost it. For forty minutes, every time I opened the mike to do a break, I burst out laughing. I stayed away from the 'Ant Hill Music' the rest of the evening, relying on Ella, Sarah and those kinds of people.

"Brother Asaiah passed away a couple of years ago. I miss him and his calls. But, he left something behind. His phrase, 'Ant Hill Music,' has lived on, as I have quoted him often via the Internet and other media. He and that phrase were one of a kind."

(D.J. Success Story)

WMAK, Nashville, Tennessee, was the first station in the radio-TV group that would be known as LIN Broadcasting.

In 1962, it had just made the switch from middle of the road to "top 40." The morning disc jockey was Ken Knight.

Then, as now, the trick to being a successful disc jockey was attracting attention. The "game plans" used then seem very tame in comparison to some of the things done now.

When Knight opened his show at six o'clock, he announced that he was going on strike to get a raise. He told his listeners that the station was giving away thousands of dollars worth of prizes. He saw no reason it couldn't afford to give him a $25.00 a week raise. He told the audience he was locking his studio door and would not unlock it until he got his raise.

To get under management's skin and to get the audience's attention, he started playing Kenny Dino's recording of "Your 'Ma' Said, You Cried In Your Sleep Last Night." It was played over and over and over. The impromptu event, which everybody connected with the station claimed no prior knowledge, continued until 9:15 that night—15¼ hours. By then, station officials and "Knight" had had enough. They gave him his raise and regular programming resumed with another disc jockey.

When Ken exited the Maxwell House Hotel, where the studios were then located, there were hundreds of cheering fans on hand, including a contingent of students from a private school in the suburbs who'd commandeered the school's bus.

Even though they thought a lot of "Ken" on the air, the Lin Broadcasting leadership moved him off the air to head their successful venture into cable TV. "Ken" changed his name back to his given name, Russell Withers, and started his own radio-TV chain. It's still in business today.

(Halloween Special)

For years at WLEC, Sandusky, Ohio, program director Karl Bates read Edgar Allen Poe stories on Halloween. Bates called himself, "your master of suspense." After he read the sponsor's ad, the announcer on duty turned the program back to Karl by announcing, "And again Karl Master Bates."

(Merry Christmas)

At the former KIKM, Sherman, Texas, a tired sounding Santa Claus was delivering weak "ho-ho-hos," imploring listeners to visit his sponsor's "Christmas Sale." The cynical disc jockey on duty told listeners, "Santa needs a laxative or a new 'hoer.'" The following day, the disc jockey needed a new job.

(A Robot)

When Johnny Cee walked into the control room, another disc jockey was on the air. Johnny was scratching himself in an inappropriate place. The on-duty disc jockey asked him what he was doing. Johnny replied, "I'm scratching my nuts." Just then, he noticed the microphone was on. He quickly added, "And bolts. Beep! Beep! I'm a robot."

(Ego Buster)

"And now it's time for one of the Midwest's most popular and versatile disc jockeys, Merv Pockins." That should be, "most popular and versatile disc jockeys, Merv Perkins."

(Saying Good-Bye)

He couldn't make up his mind at the end of his show. Should he say, "That's the whole shebang" or "That's the whole kit and caboodle"? He compromised: "the whole shittincaboodle."

Kermit Shafer
Prize Bloopers (Avenel)

THE MISS PARADE

Our all-time "Top 40" list of the worst intros, song titles, or songs:

1. Metropolitan Opera singer Anna Moffo will sing "The Star Spangled Banana."

2. Next, that all-time favorite, "A Hard Man is Good to Find." (A GOOD MAN IS HARD TO FIND)

3. At Christmastime, "Here's O Come All Ye Faithful" by Adeste Fidelis.

4. Here's the "49th Street Bridge" by Harper's Brassiere. (HARPER'S BAZAAR)

5. JONI MITCHELL sings, "You Told Me On The Radio."

6. Now, Nelson Rivers with Moon Riddles. (NELSON RIDDLE WITH MOON RIVER)

7. "Life Is a Rock, but Radio Rolled Me" by Reunion

8. The following is for a lady who just had a baby at St. Luke's Hospital. It's from her husband, "I Didn't Know The Gun Was Loaded."

9. Here's a knocked up virgin of an old favorite. (KNOCK OUT VERSION)

10. Almost 70 years ago, legendary announcer Ben Grauer made the following announcement on the network broadcast of the New York Philharmonic Orchestra: "The orchestra under the baton of Atoseo Touramini—That's Arturo Toscanini. This is your

announcer Ben Grauer. Remember that name Ben Grauer. You may never hear it again."

11. Here's the big bust out of Bayou Country, Boobie Gentry. (BOBBIE GENTRY)

12. I'm sending out the next song to my friend, Henry, and his expectant bride.

13. And now for all you newlywed ladies, "It Only Hurts for A Little While."

14. Now for a favorite selection by George Gershwin and his lovely wife, Ira.

15. Next "Heatwave" by Martha and the Vandals. (That should be Martha and the Vandellas.)

16. "Now, Keep on Pushin" by the Oppressions—I mean Impressions.

17. We regret we will not be able to bring you the service from Saint Joseph's Cathedral. Please enjoy this musical interlude, beginning with "Heaven Can Wait."

18. Before our next song, this item of local interest. Forty-two babies were born last night at Municipal Hospital. Now, "Don't Blame Me."

19. Now, here's Gary Lewis and the Playballs—I mean, Playboys.

20. Next, "Be My Wife's Companion." I mean, "Be My Life's Companion."

21. A new one: "Fifty Ways to Love Your Liver"—that should be "Love Your Lover."

22. "W O L D" by Harry Chapin

23. Next, Dolly Parton who's been nominated for an Emmy for two supporting roles.

24. Now I'm going to play "Forbidden Games." I mean the instrumental version of "Forbidden Games."

25. Next, music by Sterile Stapelton—I mean Cyril Stapelton.

26. Polka Time! In the 1950s, one of Decca Records' recording stars was Whoopie John. His given name appeared on his Record label, "John Wilfhart." A young announcer in Wisconsin polka country announced, "John Wilfhart and his Orchestra will play."

27. Here's Gladys Knight and the Pimps—I mean Pips.

28. Now all you surfers, "Grab your broads and ride, ride, ride." (SHOULD HAVE BEEN BOARDS)

29. Maybe the worst record ever made: "FM! No Static At All," by Steely Dan.

30. From Butch Cassidy and the Sundance Kid, "Raindrops Keep Falling on My Bed." (HEAD)

31. Here a song from Mama Cass Elliot's new album, "Mama's Big Ones." (Off mike, "That's a mouthful.")

32. Now, a lovely song from Josh Logan's "Fanny."

33. Here's a medley: "I'm Walking Behind You," "Finger of Suspicion," and "The Call of the Wild Goose."

34. Here's Little Willie John and "Sleep, Sleep, Sleep." Did you get any last night?

35. A special musical treat, Arthur Pops and The Boston Fiedler.

36. It's the horny sound of Al Hirt. I mean, it's the sound of Al Hirt's horn.

37. Back in the early 1950s, there was a young boy who appeared every Christmas season on the radio, singing, "I Saw Mommy Kissin' Santa Claus." Lexington disc jockey Paul Cowley had a standard outro for the record, "Shouldn't that kid be in school?"

38. Another disc jockey in the area who was going through a divorce threatened to write a country song titled, "One Has My Heart—the Other Has My Pocketbook."

39, 40. In New York City in the early 1950s, WNEW's morning team, Rayburn and Finch, were bested in the ratings by John Gambling on WOR. The duo wanted to impress the music industry with their singular abilities to promote records. They asked a publisher to give them the two worst songs in their files. They played "Music Music Music" and "Hop Scotch Polka" five times a day each. Shortly, both "worst" songs showed up on the "charts."

POLITICS

A couple of times a year, the airwaves fill up with politicians and their messages. In smaller communities where political image makers are generally not active, much of the campaigning on the air seems old fashioned; the majority of the office seekers are operating on their own—it's real, retail politics. The result is often funny. Examples:

(Cut Loose)

In a small town in the border states, a local barber several times offered himself for local office.

He appeared on various radio stations "Meet the Candidates" shows. People don't remember what he said, but they all remember his self-authored slogan, "Cut Loose and Vote For Goose."

(It Was a Lark)

In another town, not far away, a local character showed up on the ballot in the primary contest for sheriff. One of his friends bet him he wouldn't do it. He did not get a lot of votes, but "livened up" what otherwise would have been a boring contest. When he appeared on the local radio station's talk show, here's what happened:

Host: "Is it true that your family tried to have you committed?"

Candidate: "Oh, my wife did that. When we got to court, the judge told my wife, 'If you put up with that, you should be committed.'"

Listener: "Is it true that you used to run a House of ill repute on North Street?"

Candidate: "I used to live on North Street. I don't know what my wife does when I'm away from home."

(In the Deep South)

The local sheriff was accused of using county gasoline in his personal car for his personal use. The local radio station reported that and editorialized against it. The station operator started referring to the sheriff on the air as "High Octane." When it was found out that the sheriff's son, who was on the payroll, was also using county gasoline for his personal use, the station owner reported it, calling the son, "Low Octane."

(Long Shot)

In a border state primary, a candidate pundit, called the "darkest horse since Black Beauty," showed up on the ballot, campaigning on a platform of more benefits for the "middle class." He wrote his own campaign song, "Put the Jam on the Lower Shelf."

(When the People Have Spoken)

After the election is over, the local station carries the concession announcements as part of the election returns coverage. Most losing candidates are graceful in their remarks. Examples:

"I want to thank my opponent for conducting a clean race. I'm sure he'll say the same thing about me. We did not lie about each other. More important, neither of us stooped to telling the truth about each other."

RADIO POLITICIANS

(He Sang His Way into the Governor's Mansion)

He had a million-selling record in 1942. "You Are My Sunshine" was also the favorite song of King George VI of England. He appeared in three movies. He started his career on KWKH, Shreveport, Louisiana, in 1925. In 1944, he was elected governor. He was again elected in 1960. Jimmy Davis lived to be 101.

(Pass the Biscuits Pappy)

He shouldn't have had a chance. He was born in Eastern Ohio. He was raised in Kansas. His political leanings were Republican in a very Democratic state. He wasn't even registered to vote when he announced for governor in 1938. He was known and loved all over the state, thanks to his daily noontime broadcasts on six powerful Texas radio stations. He emceed a hillbilly band, read poems he personally wrote, and he did the ads for his company "Hillbilly Flour."

W.D. "Pappy" O'Daniel was not only elected governor, but also sales of "Hillbilly Flour" increased over 40% during the campaign. He kept in touch with his constituents by broadcasting every Sunday morning from the living room of the governor's mansion. He was reelected, and then won a short term and a full term in the U.S. Senate.

That's a record four statewide wins in four years, including the only statewide defeat Lyndon Johnson ever suffered.

(Fiorella LaGuardia)

He mispronounced words, growled at chiselers, squealed at hecklers, and he told loan sharks to get out of town on his

Sunday afternoon radio program on the city-owned station WNYC. During a newspaper strike, Mayor Fiorello La Guardia endeared himself to young and old, reading the Sunday funnies on his program.

POLITICS ALMOST ENDED IT

Mike Wallace was working at the second radio station of his career. He was a new reader, a staff announcer, and radio actor on such WXYZ-originated network programs as "The Green Hornet."

Harold Ickes, a member of President Franklin Roosevelt's cabinet, was in Detroit to make a major address. WXYZ carried it live. The Michigan State Network, part of the operation, was to carry it delayed to stations out in the state.

Wallace was on staff announcing duty when the recording was broadcast on the state network. An impromptu party had broken out in the corridor outside Mike's studio. After he introduced the transcription, he went outside to join the party.

In Mike's absence, the needle on the turntable got stuck. A dozen times, radio listeners heard Ickes saying, "Moe Annenberg is one of the most corrupt. Moe Annenberg is one of the most corrupt. (12 times total) Mike hurried in and dislodged the tone arm, and the program continued without a problem for the remainder of the speech.

When his shift ended, Mike was grateful that a dreaded phone call had not come in from the station's feared president, George Trendle. Mike left for New England where he was to be married and to honeymoon. When he arrived at the honeymoon hotel, there was a copy of *Time Magazine* telling about the Detroit incident.

When Mike returned to WXYZ, there was a message to "See Mr. Trendle, IMMEDIATELY."

When he did, Trendle asked him what had happened. He told him. Then Trendle said, matter of factly, "You just got married. You need the job. Go back to work."

Wallace shortly left Detroit for Chicago where he landed a continuing role in a network soap opera—a big advancement in his career, which took him 20 years later to "Sixty Minutes."

From *Close Encounters*
Mike Wallace's memoir
(William Morrow)

(The Weekend the President Was Killed)

It is a singular event in the life of every person living at that time—particularly radio people. Do you remember where you were?

In 1962, the Montana Power Company was running a radio campaign in all of its markets that featured brief renditions of songs that were popular during World War II and immediately after. When the on-duty announcer at KGVO, Missoula, read the United Press bulletin announcing that President John F. Kennedy has been shot in Dallas, the very next thing that came on the air was one of those power company spots opened by "Praise the Lord and Pass the Ammunition." It was difficult for the station boss, a well-known Republican, to convince people it was "strictly accidental."

History of Montana Broadcasting
C. Howard McDonald (Big M)

In Eastern Kentucky, Russ Hatter was just starting his radio career. He was working Sunday morning at WGOH, Grayson. A mountain preacher was delivering his radio sermon. His eyes were closed. The bell on the wire machine signaled that a bulletin was being received. When Hatter got it, he could not get the preacher's attention, so he faded him down, read the bulletin that Lee Harvey Oswald had been assassinated by Jack Ruby, and then faded him back up. The preacher finished his sermon. He got up from the studio table, put on his hat, waved goodbye and left, oblivious to the fact that he'd been interrupted for breaking news.

SPORTS MISCELLANY

(I'll Tell You No Lies)

Dennis Rappaport, boxing manager, explaining his silence regarding boxer Thomas Hearns. "I don't want to tell you any half truths unless they're completely accurate."

*

(Nothing Serious)

Boxer Alan Miuter in a radio interview said, "Sure, there have been injuries and deaths in boxing, but none of them serious."

*

(What It Takes to be a Champ)

Johnny Walker, middleweight wrist wrestling champion, told a radio audience, "It's about 90% strength and 40% technique."

*

(Who's to Blame)

A radio announcer asked Barry Beck, New York Ranger, "Who caused a brawl that broke out during the Stanley Cup Playoffs?"

"We have only one person to blame. That's each other."

*

(Dropping His Shorts)

A golf broadcaster during a tournament: "Arnie (Palmer), usually a great putter, seems to be having trouble with his long putt. However, he's having no trouble dropping his shorts."

* John's Sports Bloopers
On the "Web"

(Classic)

Frosty Mitchell and Jim Zabel each year broadcast the State Championship in Iowa Girls Basketball. One of the girl players went on a scoring rampage. Zabel said, "That girl is getting hot." Colorman Mitchell added, "They better put a good man to man on her."

Frosty's Daughter
Dorea Potter
KWON/KYFM/KRIG/KPGM
Bartlesville, Oklahoma

(Broadcasting Something Inappropriate)

Among the most popular programs on KVAK at Valdez, Alaska, are the interviews with returning fishermen. Some of the programs are even rebroadcast in Fairbanks, where her husband operates a branch of his Valdez sporting goods store.

The interviews are broadcast live. When a fisherman, his son and grandson complained on the air that there wasn't much to do in Valdez, Laurie Prax suggested, "Three good looking men, like you, should have no trouble meeting some nice ladies." To which the grandfather replied, "The women in Valdez are so ugly, even the tide wouldn't take them out."

A woman called wanting the FCC's number to complain. Laurie gave it to her. She and some visitors at the station found the incident very funny. The lady didn't lodge her FCC complaint; however, Laurie says, "I now limit my questions on the 'Fishing' program to fishing."

Lauri Prax
KVAK, Valdese, Alaska

(Fixed)

Paul Hemmer of Radio Dubuque in Iowa remembers, "Back in 1957, we had to carry the Chicago White Sox afternoon games recorded a half hour earlier because of a conflict with our locally sponsored and widely followed Noon News. One of our engineers did a masterful job of rigging it up."

Paul continues, "One of our enterprising salesmen heard the live broadcast at the station and then stopped at a nearby bar. The patrons there were listening to the recorded broadcast on WDBQ. Our salesman offered to bet on the 'Sox' to win the game. He got several takers.

"It was one of those come-from-behind storybook finishes with the 'Sox' coming from behind to win," he says. "The salesman cleaned up.

"The word got out at the station, and the manager really chewed him out, but," Hemmer muses, "I don't think he made him pay the money back."

(A Couple of Sports Broadcast Oldies but Goodies)

The radio race announcer was handed a note that the owner of a horse named "Harass" had taken her out of the next race. On the air, he told listeners to "Scratch Harass."

And in a city with four municipal golf courses, there was an annual citywide ladies golf championship. The radio announcer introduced the winner as the city's "intercourse champion."

FROM THE RADIO SPORTS SCRAPBOOK

(Boxing—Dangerous for Announcers Too)

The brawling Dempsey–Firpo fight was the first great radio fight. Firpo was knocked down seven times in Round #1 of the October 1923 bout. Dempsey was knocked through the ropes and outside the ring, landing on top of announcer Graham McNamee.

After the fight, McNamee said, "My heart was thumping at my breast until I thought it would break my ribs."

(At the Track)

He had been around horses all his life. His father was a veterinary dentist. He worked for both national racing sheets. He became loudspeaker announcer at Bowie Race Course in 1923. He joined NBC in 1929. His gravel voice and folksy style were familiar to everyone.

Clem McCarthy was pushed into service on radio at the Kentucky Derby. The man, who was supposed to call it, had bet on an earlier race. He called it wire-to-wire for his favorite, WHO LOST, causing the betting broadcaster to end with, "You son of a bitch."

In 1947, near the end of his career, McCarthy got mixed up while calling the "Preakness." He called the race for "Jet Pilot." He lost track of the real winner, "Faultless," during the stretch.

(In the Ring Too)

Clem was also very good on boxing. He brought America the 1938 first-round victory of Joe Louis over Germany's "great hope," Max Schmeling. It is still considered a broadcast classic.

UNCLE DON

(He Didn't Do It)

I hope you've enjoyed reading these funny radio stories, as much as I've enjoyed telling them. I feel obligated, at this point, to put an end to the telling of one of radio's oldest yarns—the Uncle Don blooper.

The story has been passed along from generation to generation ever since the late 1920s, when the incident was said to have occurred.

Uncle Don was born Howard Rice in 1897 at St. Joseph, Michigan, across Lake Michigan from Chicago. During his teens, he joined the circus as an acrobat. By fifteen, he was on stage in vaudeville and in drama playing stock Irishman parts. He gained some notoriety as a trick piano player, able to play while standing on his head.

He worked as an announcer, vocal handyman, and "stand by" pianist at New York radio stations WMCA and WOR. A toy manufacturer came into WOR and asked for a demonstration of a children's show it might sponsor. Don Carney, as he had been known for years, quickly put something together. The sponsor liked it and bought it. "Uncle Don" on radio debuted in 1928 and ran into 1947—almost 20 years. The program consisted of original stories, songs, jokes, advice, birthday announcements, personal messages, club news, and a lot of commercials. After its run on WOR, "Uncle Don" did as so many New Yorkers do, he decided to spend his senior years in sunny Florida. He did his show on WKAT, Miami, until his death in 1954.

The Urbanlegends.com site did extensive investigations of the "Uncle Don" story and found it not to be true.

Legend has it that after finishing his program, he leaned back in his chair, not knowing his microphone was still on, and said (to himself), "There, that ought to hold the little bastards." The legend continues that Uncle Don was fired and a soundalike hired to take his place. NONE OF THIS was reported in general circulation newspapers or the trade press. It surely would have been—had it been true.

It may have happened somewhere else where someone doing a similar program lapsed. There were "Uncles" and "Aunts" in almost every radio market in the United States—large and small.

At WDLB, Marshfield, Wisconsin, Bob Behling, the station's general manager, was on the radio for a regional bakery on Saturday morning doing the "Uncle Bob Show."

Some people claim they heard the "Uncle Don" remark on the air. They are obviously mistaken. Actually, many years later, when Kermit Shafer included it on one of his "bloopers" record albums, he admitted he had hired an actor to play "Uncle Don" uttering the words that damaged his reputation. Kermit apologized and admitted hiring the actor.

(He Did It, But)

"Ladies and Gentlemen, the President of the United States, Hoobert Heever." That's one of the longest running "radio blooper" broadcasting lore. In the telling and retelling, some of the facts have been altered. Chicago radio historian Chuck Schaden got the real story by talking to announcer Harry Von Zell himself. "It was not the opening of a presidential speech. It was during the closing of a CBS documentary on the president's life and career. I had delivered the president's name at least 20 times correctly, earlier in the program."

IT SLIPPED

Here are some odds 'n' ends that did not easily fit into the earlier parts of this book. Some of them kind of came to mind from personal experience (sometimes painful) and from people who were nice enough to share them with me.

(What's in a Name)

His real name is David Holler (not made up or a radio name). He came to work as a part-time announcer when Kevin and Dorea Potter bought WMOI, Monmouth, Illinois, in 1982. (They sold it some years later.)

Mr. Holler made things very uncomfortable when he opened the local obituaries portion of the local news with, "These people are dying to make the news." The young man's career in radio was short.

(What a Year)

The Midland Advertising Agency had a long association with radio, beginning in its very earliest days. They had what now would be called "A Local Marketing Agreement" in the mid 1920s with WKRC in Cincinnati where both entities are located.

When prohibition ended, Midland Advertising Agency won the Burger Brewing Company's advertising account. It was Midland that forged the beer's quarter century association with Cincinnati Reds baseball.

Every year, Midland came up with a memorable slogan for its client. One of the very best got twisted by a local announcer on a Burger sports program. He said that the program was sponsored by Burger, "A finer year beer after beer." The slogan was "BURGER, A FINER BEER YEAR AFTER YEAR." The local distributor got so much needling from his friends and customers that he made sure the program was renewed year after year.

(Hits the Spot)

One of my advertisers, a local bank, had added trust services. On their newscast, an announcer told listeners that the bank's chief executive officer was ready to serve as "executer" instead of "executor." A former judge, the bank's CEO, said that a lot of people came in to see him, wanting to know "exactly what I did."

(Who's That)

The announcer on a daily devotional program read the prepared opening, but when he got to the blanks where the guest minister and his church were to be inserted, he forget the name of the minister and his church. This happened not just once, but twice. The third day, the minister showed up with a sign he'd made out of a laundry shirt card. On it, he printed his name and his church. He held the card up as he was being introduced.

(They Understood)

Linda B (that's her air name) wrote from Ketchikan, Alaska, where she's on the air at KTKT and KGTW. Her program was so busy one morning that when she answered the phone, she told the caller, "Please be patient while I catch my breast."

(It Rhymes)

One of the best announcers I ever worked with, or worked

for me, was Irv Miller. He was at WDLB, Marshfield, Wisconsin, where I started out.

He seldom fluffed. When he did, it was "a beaut." A local department store was having a sale on "Blue Bell Overhauls." Irv called them "Blue Balls Overhauls." He was philosophical about it saying, "It Rhymes."

(Where Is It)

WDLB had two announcers with the same first name, Irv Miller and Erv Kult. One relieved the other at two o'clock each afternoon. There was a shoe store commercial on the break. Before an H. and S. Shoe Store commercial was read, the announcer blew a police whistle. One day, when Miller sat down to do the commercial, he couldn't find the whistle. Over the air, he said, "Where the hell's the H. and S. whistle?" Kult reached into the wastebasket, where it had accidentally been dropped.

That was in 1952. Every management person in the building headed into the announcer's booth. The telephone started ringing with complaints. The following few days, some angry mail came in including a letter from Madison, the state capital, far outside WDLB's 250-watt coverage area. For thirty days, the management anxiously waited for a citation from the FCC. When none came within the month, everybody breathed a sigh of relief. How times have changed.

(Slipped Right Out of a Job)

Since it went on the air twenty years before, KMA, Shenandoah, Iowa, was a big station in a small town and enjoyed a lot of prestige.

In the summer of 1941, the station hired a young college boy to work the evening shift. It was easy duty, because KMA carried the NBC-Blue Network. All the announcer did, normally, was read the station breaks. There was one exception: a fifteen-minute non-network program of songs by Dinah Shore.

The young college boy introduced the program, and then leaned back in his chair. He cracked his funny bone on the edge of a turntable and let out a yell, "JESUS CHRIST ON A BLOODY CRUTCH." He had forgotten to turn his microphone off.

The telephone from the transmitter rang, and the engineer said the "off color" yell had gone out over the air. The next afternoon when he arrived at the station, there was an envelope telling him he'd been fired, effective immediately.

The young man quickly found another job at KORN (later KHUB), Fremont, Nebraska. Within ten years of being fired at KMA, Alan Baumgaard was host of one of the upper Midwest's most popular and highest billing programs, "The Housewives Protective League" on CBS-owned and operated WCCO, Minneapolis/Saint Paul. At this writing, he is the founder/owner/chairman of KLKS, Breezy Point, Minnesota, in the Brainard market. During his 65 years on the air, he's been known to legions of fans as Alan Gray.

(I'm Not Going)

I'm indebted to Bill Hartnett, a longtime radio and sometime television guy, who's retired now in Cincinnati and is enjoying a great career in community theatre.

During my years in broadcasting and during the months gathering material for this book, I've never heard a story that tops this one.

Bill Hartnett was the news director of WGR, Buffalo, during a format change. The general manager fired a fellow named John who was doing a talk show. He or his show wouldn't be needed after the format change, but John refused to be fired. He told the manager, "This is my home. You cannot fire me. I'll sweep the floors, empty the trash cans, make the coffee." He spent eight or more hours every day doing whatever he could do to stay busy.

Hartnett soon successfully lobbied the manager for permission to hire John in the news department. It happened at exactly the right time for WGR. One of the biggest stories in the region's history broke out, and John proved himself invaluable. It was the prisoner standoff at the Attica State Prison less than 30 miles away. John ingratiated himself to everyone during that event, so that when he did leave WGR, he left on his terms and at his time.

(Parting Words)

An announcer on a station in the Midwest obviously had too much "holiday spirit" when he told his listeners "On behalf of all the personnel here at the radio station, I wish you season's greetings and a very happy and Preposterous new year."

INDEX

A

Albright, Abe, 83
Algood, Eddie, 71
Allan, Mark, 46, 103
Allegood, Wandell, 71
Announcer Audition, 67
Ant Hill Music, 124

B

Baker, Todd, 61
Barber, Red, 25
Bates, Karl, 126
Beck, Barry, 138
Behling, Bob, 144
Belcher, Jerry, 3
Bell, Jack, 105
Bellinger, Steve, 48
Bergen and McCarthy, 31
Berra, Yogi, 24
Billings, Dick and Pat, 19, 117
Black, Jerry, 56
Block, Martin, 122
Blodgett, Esther, 74
Bohannon, Jim, 11
Boone, Bob, 25
Brandt, John, 89
Braswell, Jay, 22
Brinkley, Chris, 120
Brinkley, John R., 36, 37
Brooks, Garth, 18
Brown, Curt, 82
Burdon, Don, 115
Burger Beer, 24, 145
Burton, Don 121

C

Caldwell, Dewey, 66
Cannon, Steve, 99
Carney, Don (see Uncle Don) 140
Carroll, Jim, 98
Carver, Walker, 75
Cashion, John, 20
CBS, 92
Cee, Johnny, 127
Charles, Antell, 38
Charles, Rick, 76
Clear Channel Communications, 89
Cooley, Art, 96
Cooley, Denny, 54, 94
Cowley, Paul, 131
Crain, Bill, 81

D

Davidson, Jim, 74
Davis, Jimmy (Gov.), 134
Dean, Dizzy, 26
Dillinger, John, 112
Dimmit, Bob, 94
Dodd, Skeeter, 16, 65
Doran, Kevin, 17
Dorsey, Terry, 39
Drobney, Howard, 72

E

Eastman, George, 34
Eigen, Jack, 8

F

Franken, Al, 12
French, Ray, 52
Fuller, Gary, 73

Funt, Allen, 107

G

Gallagher, Mike, 12
Gambling, John, 131
Geller, Valarie, 49
Ghrist, John Russell, 112
Godfrey, Arthur, 84
Goldberg, Mel, 82
Gooding, Fred, 110
Gowdy, Curt, 24
Grauer, Ben, 128
Gray, Alan, 147
Gray, Barry, 8
Green Bay Packers, 52
Greer, Ralph, 75, 101
Grizzard, Ted, 1, 5, 19

H

Hadacol, 38
Hammer Beverages, 63
Hannity, Sean, 11
Harrell, Bill, 19, 55
Harris, John, iii
Hartnett, Bill, 83, 148
Hatter, Russ, 109, 117, 137
Hedges, Howard, 124
Hemmer, Paul, 140
Henderson, Carlisle, 68
Henderson, W.K., 33
Hiney Wine, 39
Hodges, Paul, 5
Holbrook, Ray, 119
Holler, David, 145
Howard, Paul, 44
Hoyt, Waite, 24

I

Imus, Don, 13, 85
Ingraham, Laura, 13

J

Jarvis, Al, 123
Jindra, Joe, 119
Johnson, Parks, 3

K

Kallinger, Paul, 36
Kapp, Jack, 122
Kasper, Vern, 79
Kennedy, John, 93
Kennedy, John F., 137
King, Larry, 85
Knight, Frances, 41
Kokash, Jim, 71
Krebsbach, Ed, 121
Kult, Erv, 147

L

LaGuardia, Fiorella, 134
Land, Allan, 81
Landers, Ann, 115
Lemense, Phil, 103
Liddy, G. Gordon, 13
Limbaugh, Rush, 11, 13, 87
Lin Broadcasting, 125
Linda B, 146
Livesay, Ray, 14
Lockhardt, Ray, 89
Long, Larry, 22
Love, Betty, 105
Luther, T. David, 48

M

McCarthey, Clem, 142
McDonald, C. Howard, 56, 121, 135
McDougal, Mike, 76
McIntyre, John, 30
McLendon, Gordon, 35, 40, 97
McNamee, Graham, 142

McNeil, Don, 50
Mack, Bill, 6, 38
Marconi Awards, 100
Martin, Don, 43, 80
Martin, Slim, 65
May, Walter, 83
Metheney, Terry, 95
Metzger, Earl, 80
Miller, Irv, 147
Mitchell, Frosty, 97, 139
Morgan, Archie, 55
Morganruth, Earl, 18
Mullins, Paul "Moon", 74

N

Nash, Francis, 15, 65
National Enquirer, v
NBC, 102
New Hampshire Broadcasters Assn., 80
Nochman, Gerald, 67

O

Oakley, Billie, 100
Obler, Arch, 31
O'Daniel, W.D. "Pappy", 134
Olsen, Doug, 69
Olsen, Paul, 81
Osborn, Ed, 101
Osborn, Elize, 101
Owens, Don, 60

P

Palmer, Arnold, 139
Patterson, Tommy, 78
Pearce, Houston, 82
Perkins, Merv, 127
Phillips, Wally, 85
Pope, Generoso, iv
Post, Cincinnati, iv
Potter, Kevin and Dorea, 145

Prax, Laurie, 46, 139
Price, Basil, 14
Pyne, Joe, 10

Q

Quaal, Ward, 85

R

Radent, Ken, 38
Ramar (Crystal Ball Gazer), 114
Raney, Rex, 66
Rayburn and Finch, 131
Reagan, Ronald, 87
Rogers, Bob, 105
Rolling, Jim, 102
Russell, Charlie, 22

S

Savage, Mike, 12
Schieffer, Bob, 92
Schultz, Ed, 12
Sellers, Rick, 113
Shaden, Chuck, 144
Sherman, Bob, i
Shetley, Don, 68
Schlessinger, Dr. Laura, 84
Smith, H. Allen, 102
Sorenson, Dean I, 16, 69
Spradlin, Bob, 111
Springer, Jerry, 12
Squires, Ken, 60
Stanton, Harry Dean, 119
Steele, Bob, 63
Stoner, Jim, 42
Stratton, Charlie, 109
Suglia, Joe, 18
Sutton, Art, i

T

Taylor, Bill, 20
Thomas, Lowell, 113
Thompson, Jim, 69
Tinkle, Paul, 120
Tisinger, Judge Bob, 33
Tobey, Cliff, 44
Tomlinson, Bob, 4
Trivers, Steve, ii
Tucker, Dale, 40
Tyrone, Pennsylvania, 108

U

Uecker, Bob, 27
Uncle Don, 143

V

Vito, Lou, 42, 106
Vox Pop, 2

W

Wallace, Mike, v, 136
War of the Worlds, 108
Warren, Tony, 118
Webb, Tom, 4, 118
Weinert, Phil, 78
Weldy, Dan, 42
Wells, Orson, 108
Wertz, Bill, ii
West, Mae, 31
Widsen, Hal, 44, 115
Wigglesworth, Carl Truman, 89
Wilfart, John, 130
Williams, Armstrong, 13
Williams, Jerry, 9
Willis, Bill (Colonel), 60
Wills, Bob, 6
Wilson, Bob, 115
Withers, Russ, 125
WKRP in Cincinnati, 147
Wolfman Jack, 37
Wonder, Stevie, 32
Woolley, Lynn, 99

Z

Zappa, Frank, 10

INDEX OF STATIONS BY CALL LETTERS

KABL, San Francisco, CA, 35
KADS, Los Angeles, CA, 35
KAHL, San Antonio, TX, 89
KAKI, San Antonio, TX, 35
KBBC, Lake Havasu, AZ, 32
KBBI, Homer AK, 124
KCLY, Clay Center, KS, 119
KDLM, Detroit Lakes, MN, 72
KEEL, Shreveport, LA, 35
KERV, Kerrville, TX 23
KEVA, Shamrock, TX, 6
KFBK, Sacramento, CA, 87
KFWB, Hollywood, CA, 122
KGB, San Diego, CA, 35
KGCX, Wolfe Point, MT, 121
KGDE (now KBRF), Fergus Falls, MN, 72
KGNO, Dodge City, KS, 33
KGRN, Grinnell, IA, 97
KGVO, Missoula, MT, 137
KGW, Seattle, WA, 4
KHAS, Hastings, NE, 71
KICY, Nome, AK, 32
KIKM, Sherman, TX, 127
KILO, Colorado Springs, CO, 32
KILT, Houston, TX 35
KISS, San Antonio, TX, 44
KJLH, Los Angeles, CA, 32
KLEM/KZZL, LaMars, IA, 81
KLIF, Dallas, TX, 35
KLYK, Longview, WA, 61
KMA, Shenendoah, IA, 34, 147
KMBZ, Kansas City, MO, 87
KMPC, Los Angeles, CA, 29

KMRY, Cedar Rapids, IA, 113
KNCK/KCKS Concordia, KS, 119
KOBH, Hot Springs, SD, 69
KOGA, Ogalala, NE, 89
KOIL, Omaha, NE, 115
KONO, San Antonio, TX, 89
KORN (now KHUB) Fremont, NE, 147
KORN, Mitchell, SD, 16
KQV, Pittsburgh, PA, 87
KSCS, Dallas, TX, 39
KSEN, Shelby, MT, 56
KSJO, San Jose, CA, 47
KSLO/KOGM, Opelousas, LA, 71
KTKS, Breezy Point, MN, 147
KTKT/KGTW, Ketchikan, AK, 146
KTRH, Houston, TX, 2
KTSA, San Antonio, TX, 35
KTTS, Springfield, MO, 82
KUTY, Palmdale, CA, 23
KVAK, Valdese, AK, 104, 139
KVOA/KOYE, Laredo, TX, 19, 55
KVOP, Plainview, TX, 55
KWAT, Watertown, SD, 72
KWKH, Shreveport, LA, 33 134
KWRT AM/FM, Boonville, MO, 19, 117
WABC, New York, NY, 50
WAOP, Otsego, MI (now WAKV), 22

155

WARL/WAVA, Arlington, VA, 60
WATD, Marshfield, MA, 33
WBAT, Marion, IN, 64
WBBM, Chicago, IL, 10
WBCH, Hastings, MI, 38
WBCU, Union, SC, 68, 101
WBNZ, Frankfort, MI, 54
WBTM, Danville, VA, 34, 71
WBYE, Calera, AL, 53
WBZ, Boston, MA, 10
WCAU, Philadelphia, PA 35
WCAW, Charleston, WV, 44, 66
WCBQ, Oxford, NC, 35
WCCO, Minneapolis, MN, 147
WCHK, Canton, GA, 76
WCMT, Martin, TN, 120
WCPO, Cincinnati, OH (now WDBZ), 85
WCSI, Columbus, IN, 2
WCVL, Crawfordsville, IN, 52
WCYN, Cynthiana, KY, iii, 89
WDAD, Indiana, PA, 33
WDBQ, Dubuque, IA, 140
WDEV, Waterbury, VT, 60
WDLB, Marshfield, WI, 114, 146
WDVA, Danville, VA, 71
WDZ, Decatur, IL, 48
WEKY, Richmond, KY, 2
WESR, Olney, VA, 23
WFAN, New York, NY, 13, 85
WFHG, Bristol, VA, 66
WFKY, Frankfort, KY, 110, 117
WFLQ, French Lick, IN, 60
WFTG, London, KY, 34
WFTM, Maysville, KY, 34

WGCD, Chester, SC, 20
WGEL, Greenville, IL, 93
WGN, Chicago, IL, 85
WGOG, Walhalla, SC, 35
WGOH/WUGO, Grayson, KY, 15
WHAM, Rochester, NY, 34
WHIZ, Zanesville, OH, 81
WHKP, Hendersonville, NC, 96
WHO, Des Moines, IA, 87
WIBG, Philadelphia, PA, 9
WILM, Wilmington, DE, 10
WIND, Gary, IN, 112
WINS, New York, NY, 8
WIOD, Miami, FL, 85
WIXE, Monroe, NC, 55 105
WIXZ (Near Pittsburgh, PA), 87
WJEF, Grand Rapids, MI (now WTKG), 85
WKAT, Miami, FL, 143
WKDW, Camden, NJ, 9
WKKR, Opelika/Auburn, AL 73
WKLX, Lexington, KY (now WLXG), 41
WKOA, Hopkinsville, KY (now WHVO), 109
WKRO, Cairo, IL, 81
WLBB, Carrollton, GA, 33
WLBC, Muncie, IN, 121
WLEA, Hornell, NY, 17
WLEC, Sandusky, OH, 126
WLOA, Braddock, PA, 63
WLW, Cincinnati, OH, 34
WMAK, Nashville, TN (now WNQM), 125
WMCA, New York, 8
WMEX, Boston, MA, 9
WMGR, Harvard, IL 74

WMIR, Lake Geneva, WI, 49
WMOG, Brunswick, GA, 33
WMOI, Monmouth, IL, 145
WMST, Mount Sterling, KY, 4, 111, 116, 118
WNEW, New York, NY, 121, 131
WNOE, New Orleans, LA, 21
WNUS, Chicago, IL (now WGRB), 35
WNYC, New York, NY, 134
WOAI, San Antonio, TX 89
WOC, Davenport, IA, 87
WOKY, Milwaukee, WI, 95
WOR, New York, NY, 131, 143
WORD, Spartanburg, SC, 20
WOWO, Fort Wayne, IN, 83
WPET, Goldsboro, NC, 65
WPKO/WBLL, Bellefontaine, OH, 42, 106
WQXC, Otsego, MI, 54
WRDS, Charleston, WV, 66
WRFC, Athens, GA, 76
WRJC, Mauston, WI, 76
WSAZ, Huntington, WV, 34
WSLM, Salem, IN, 43, 80
WSNG, Torrington, CT 32
WSUN, St. Petersburg, FL, 34
WTBF, Troy, AL, 102
WTIC, Hartford, CT, 63
WTRN, Tyrone, PA, 108
WTSB, Lumberton, NC, 34
WVLK, Lexington, KY, 118, 119
WVOP, Vidalia, GA, 5
WWNS, Statesboro, GA, 21, 33
WXYZ, Detroit, 136
WYGL, Selinsgrove, PA, 33
WYSL, Buffalo, NY (now WWWS), 35
WZMG, Opelika/Auburn, AL, 73

ORDER FORM

Individually signed copies of Bob Doll's books are available from the author

The RADIO FUNNY Book $13.95
First Class Mailing, Tax,   + 4.50
Handling $18.45 x _____ = $_____

*A Perfect Union: Union, SC
and Its Radio Station* $9.95
First Class Mailing, Tax,   + 4.50
Handling $14.45 x _____ = $_____

*Sparks Out of the Plowed Ground:
History of America's
Small Town Stations* $9.95
First Class Mailing, Tax,   + 4.50
Handling $14.45 x _____ = $_____

Bob & Barbara Doll
1746 Rosewood Street
Seguin, Texas 78155
Phone: 830 379 7549
FAX: 830 372 2905
Email: bobar@sbcglobal.net

Name _____

Address _____

_____

_____

Phone (   ) _____ - _____

Check enclosed for $_____
or charge my _____ Credit Card

_____ Exp _____